P9-ASI-245

Contents

★ ★ ★

OPERATION
FINANCIAL FREEDOM

★ ★ ★

THE ULTIMATE PLAN TO BUILD WEALTH AND
LIVE THE LIFE YOU WANT

James Dicks

JW Dicks

McGraw-Hill

New York   Chicago   San Francisco
Lisbon   London   Madrid   Mexico City   Milan
New Delhi   San Juan   Seoul   Singapore
Sydney   Toronto

1 2 3 4 5 6 7 8 9 0   DOC/DOC   0 9 8 7 6 5

ISBN 0-07-146305-4

First Edition

This publication is designed to provide accurate and
authoritative information in regard to the subject matter
covered. It is sold with the understanding that neither the
author nor the publisher is engaged in rendering legal,
accounting, or other professional service. If legal advice
or other expert assistance is required, the services of a
competent professional person should be sought.
> —*From a Declaration of Principles jointly adopted
> by a Committee of the American Bar
> Association and a Committee of Publishers*

McGraw-Hill books are available at special quantity
discounts to use as premiums and sales promotions, or for
use in corporate training programs. For more information,
please write to the Director of Special Sales, Professional
Publishing, McGraw-Hill, Two Penn Plaza, New York, NY
10121-2298. Or contact your local bookstore.

Interior book design by Arlene Lee

This book is printed on recycled, acid-free
paper containing a minimum of 50% recycled
de-inked fiber.

*To the men and women
of America's armed forces*

Success in war depends upon the golden rule of war. Speed—simplicity—boldness.

—George S. Patton

★ ★ ★

Operation Financial Freedom Explained

Risk more than others think is safe.
Care more than others think is wise.
Dream more than others think is practical.
Expect more than others think is possible.

—U.S. Military Academy cadet maxim

The United States has always been known as "the land of opportunity." While Americans sometimes take this for granted, other countries' citizens risk their very lives just to live the American Dream. Often arriving on these shores with little more than the shirts on their backs, these immigrants and refugees come to the United States with the fervent and heartfelt belief that they, too, can amass wealth in a country where the streets are "paved with gold."

Do they have enormous disadvantages to overcome and hard lessons to learn? Obviously. At the same time, though, they have one critical advantage: Unlike many Americans, these immigrants aren't jaded. They believe in the American Dream—and therefore they are willing to work incredibly hard to make it come true.

Their faith is well placed. In fact, wealth *can* still be made in America today—but only if you establish the right financial goals for yourself and are willing to work hard to achieve them.

Millions of Americans today fail on both counts. They don't set realistic goals, and they don't work hard at achieving financial freedom. Many waste money on lottery tickets and get-rich-quick schemes—despite the long odds against success, and despite the fact that even for the winners, these kinds of financial windfalls rarely lead to lasting financial success.

This book depicts achieving financial freedom as a *journey*—a trip that is likely to include obstacles and roadblocks, but that is just as likely to present pleasant surprises along the way. No, there is no path to instant riches. But there *is* a path that can help lead you to long-term success.

It's a path that James came upon indirectly, as a result of his years in the military. As a former U.S. Marine and member of the Marine Corps League, James learned early on that many of the same principles and characteristics that make you a good *soldier* can also make you a sound *investor*. For example, both investors and soldiers are likely to fail if they lack a strong sense of discipline. Similarly, they're likely to fail if they don't possess a certain amount of emotional fortitude.

As you turn the pages of this book, you will find dozens of quotes from noted military experts and other noteworthy leaders. Most of these quotes were not uttered with any thought of wealth building or financial planning. And yet, they provide ample evidence of the strong overlaps between successful *military* thinking and successful *financial* thinking.

For example, one of the most exceptional generals in modern history, George S. Patton, is quoted more than a dozen times throughout the book. In digging through papers and books detailing his life and career, we came across some very interesting notes that West Point Cadet Patton made in the margins of his copy of the textbook *Elements of Strategy*. Cadet Patton listed the six qualities of a "great general" as follows:

1. Tactically aggressive
2. Strength of character
3. Steadiness of purpose
4. Acceptance of responsibility
5. Energy
6. Good health

While those six traits may not add up to an *exact* definition of an exceptional investor, they are a very good place to start. The best investors must be aggressive (*at the right times*). They must have character, have a strong sense of purpose, accept responsibility for their decisions, and so on.

> *Only our individual faith in freedom can keep us free.*
>
> —Dwight D. Eisenhower

Throughout this book, you will find equally compelling words of wisdom and advice from noteworthy military figures (e.g., General Douglas MacArthur) and former commanders-in-chief (e.g., Dwight D. Eisenhower). Again, these words of wisdom are intended to help reinforce the key concepts that are presented in a step-by-step program in each of the three parts of the book.

In late 2004, we made a commitment as a family to embark on a special mission.

Because of James' service in and association with the military and the valuable lessons he had learned as a Marine, he had a strong desire to give something back to the men and women of the military. Coauthor (and uncle), JW Dicks, also "caught" the vision, as we both came to understand how the lessons we had learned in the financial world could be used to change the lives of millions of men and women in a positive direction.

The heroic individuals in our armed forces risk their lives to keep this country, and its way of life, safe. They fight for *our* freedom. We thought that in return, we could at least fight for their *financial* freedom. And while the financial strategies highlighted in this book are designed to help investors and financial consumers of all types, and at all income levels, we hope that military personnel and their families will find our ideas particularly useful.

Operation Financial Freedom was launched in early 2005. Its mission is to teach specific financial strategies that anyone can learn and use to become more successful. As part of our overall mission to arm military people with the tools they need to become financially free, we are offering free education and training programs to service personnel. For more information on those programs, contact www.jamesdicks.com.

If you are not in the military but seek financial freedom for yourself, we have developed a free educational site that will expand on the strategies taught in this book. You can access the site at www.jamesdicks.com.

This book continues in the same vein. It is an expansion of our gift to the men and women in our armed forces. A portion of the authors' royalties derived from this book will go directly to benefit the nonprofit Financial Freedom

We have a toolbox that's full of tools, and I brought them all to the party.

—Colin Powell

Foundation that we set up to extend the opportunities of financial freedom throughout this country.

To our readers in the military: We thank you, and we welcome you to the journey toward your own success. For those of you who are not in the military, rest assured that the information in *Operation Financial Freedom* can help you, too, as you begin your journey to financial independence.

James Dicks

JW Dicks

★ ★ ★

ACKNOWLEDGMENTS

I t is always amazing how much time and how many people it takes to produce a book like this.

We would like to thank McGraw-Hill, Inc. for its commitment to making this book the powerful message of Financial Freedom it has become. Specific thanks within its fine organization to Jeffrey Krames, vice president and publisher of the business book division. There is no question that without Jeffrey's tireless championship of this book, it would not have seen the light of day. His writing, his edits, and his salesmanship have helped make the quality product you hold in your hand. Thanks to Laura Libretti, who makes the trains run on time; Ruth Mannino, the tireless production genius who keeps track of a million details; and Lydia Rinaldi, our fantastic publicist who is already working behind the scenes to promote the book.

Thanks also to our associates at PremiereTrade™. It is truly unfortunate we can't list you all, but we do thank each of you for your contributions in making our company run and providing the type of quality financial service we give to our customers. A special thanks to Jack Lott for his help and contacts with the military.

And finally, thanks to our wives, Linda and Deb, and to our children, Jennifer, Lindsay, James, and Jacqueline. Our wives make the journey exciting, and our children provide the inspiration to pass down knowledge that has been given to us from previous generations. The circle continues.

James Dicks

JW Dicks

★ ★ ★

PART 1

Preparing for Your Mission to Wealth

Part 1 of this book focuses on getting you mentally prepared for the journey to wealth. As you will learn, being mentally ready is at least as important as anything you will do down the line. Why is your mental outlook so important? You will learn the full answer in the three chapters in Part 1, but suffice it to say that financial freedom requires more than picking mutual funds or choosing the hot stock of the moment. It involves patience, discipline, and maturity.

The other key to Part 1 involves goal setting and making sure that your values and goals are in alignment. We will ask you to complete several short exercises that will help you to understand what it is that you want for your future, assist you in identifying your priorities, and help you to create a personal mission statement. Once you have completed Part 1, you will be ready to move on to Parts 2 and 3 and to learn to master the skills and habits that will help you to achieve financial independence.

★ ★ ★

CHAPTER 1

Discover Your Financial Freedom Mindset

The journey of a thousand miles begins with a single step.

—Lao-tzu

There is an old saying that the best way to make a million dollars is to start out with two million. We thought the saying was cute, but we certainly didn't see how it applied to us in any meaningful way. Then we both lost more money than we cared to count in the real estate business.

What we learned from the experience was that financial freedom is as much a *mindset* as it is net worth. You have to think about financial freedom as a *process*—not just a goal to achieve, but an activity that you continue, and expand upon, once you have reached your goal. You have to develop a plan, implement specific strategies to make that plan a reality, and then come up with a revised plan. That is what this book is all about.

In addition to giving you concrete financial freedom strategies for achieving "tycoon" status, we have also written about the thought processes that ought to lie behind the making, keeping, and spending of your money. Why? Because without this additional understanding and discipline, the arbitrary dollar amount you may achieve won't mean a thing.

> *Happiness lies not in the mere possession of money. It lies in the joy of achievement, in the thrill of creative effort.*
> —Franklin Delano Roosevelt

At this early stage, you are probably skeptical. If so, good for you! We intend to earn your trust, step by step. For the moment, though, we ask you to suspend disbelief. Imagine that we are people whom you *know* and *believe in*, who have been there for you before and have told it to you straight in the past. That way, you'll be more open to the principles that we're going to put in front of you—some of which may sound a little unexpected, even strange.

So here's our first lesson: Your mindset is critically important. Yes, making money and achieving financial freedom is important—that's what this book is mainly about—but *getting into the right frame of mind* is at least as important. Without the proper mindset, you probably won't keep the money you make—and even if you do, you probably won't enjoy it as much as you thought you would. And, after all, *enjoying* your financial freedom is what makes that freedom worth pursuing in the first place.

Financial Freedom Strategy No. 1: Create Your Definition of Financial Freedom

Several years ago, in the best-selling book *The Millionaire Next Door*, the authors described the day-to-day lives of contemporary millionaires: what they think, what they buy, their daily habits, and so on. What came through loud and clear was a *mindset* of success. Those millionaires next door were recognizable—in other words, in lots of ways, they weren't all that different from you and me. But they *were* distinctive in the way they thought about the world, and about their wealth. Not that they were all the same—far from it. But they shared certain kinds of discipline in the way they dealt with the world.

Our goal is to help you achieve that kind of discipline, so that you can move from where you are to where you *want to be*. That means slightly different things for different people—there's no "one size fits all"—but that is the fun and beauty of financial freedom.

Wars are lost in the mind before they are lost on the ground.

—George S. Patton

Will simply reading this book give you financial freedom? Of course not. What it *can* do, though, is show you the ropes. It can explain the key principles of wealth creation and teach you strategies that you can use to achieve financial freedom. Perhaps for the first time in your life, you will have the benefit of a step-by-step process that you can follow to obtain wealth for yourself and your family.

If you let us, we will do our best to be the money mentor you have always wanted to find. We will also offer you long-term education, training, and support. So let's start by asking a few of the questions that may be on your mind as you think about trying to achieve financial freedom.

"Will it be easy?"

No. Very few things that are of value come easily. But it will be *fun*—like learning a new sport, taking up a new instrument, or learning a new language—and that is the exciting part. Planning for financial freedom, and then getting there, can be among life's most rewarding experiences.

"What is financial freedom?"

Conformity is the jailer of freedom and the enemy of growth.

—John Fitzgerald Kennedy

That's a sensible question to ask up front. The definition of financial freedom is different for everyone. For some, it is a substantial net worth, consisting of reasonably liquid assets—say, a million bucks cash in the bank. (*Liquid* simply means that it's available to you on short notice. Cash is liquid; real estate is not.) Others tie financial freedom to some level of annual income, like, a million dollars in cash, gross. Still others would raise the bar and say, "a million a year *after taxes*."

But everything's relative, and people's expectations vary widely. To you and me, a million dollars (in *any* of these flavors) is a whole lot of money. But to Bill Gates, Warren Buffett, or Donald Trump, a million dollars probably wouldn't mean all that much.

So which definition is right?

The one you pick, of course. As you turn the pages of this book, you will quickly see that the only thing that's truly important is what *you* believe. The moment you start trying to live by someone else's standards, you're likely to lose the war, even if you win some short-term battles.

As a Financial Freedom Fighter, you simply have to *set a standard for yourself.* And you must be comfortable with that standard, because you are going to have to live with it for a long time.

So, let's do it. Let's set your wealth standard. Put a bookmark here, close the book, and *think* about it for a moment. What does being financially free mean to you? Is it cash or assets? How much, or what kind? Is it a guaranteed income stream? How big? Decide for yourself, and fill in the blank in the exercise.

EXERCISE 1

Financial freedom is _____

_____

_____

_____

Was that a painful exercise? If not, good; you're probably in a good mindset to start planning for your financial freedom. If it *was* painful, well, don't worry too much about that. Part of what this book intends to do is to help you get to the right definitions. And by the way, there's a very good chance that you'll want to revisit and change your definition as you learn more about our principles and philosophy.

In fact, in later chapters, we'll ask you to answer the same question again, in writing. Why? In part to help you see how your thinking is evolving. But also, we believe strongly that *writing things down* is a form of commitment to those ideas. It makes the ideas take a more concrete form—words on a page, in black and white—and become a part of you.

Here's a tough one: *Why* do you want to become financially free?

Maybe that doesn't sound so tough, at first blush. But believe us, it's not as simple as it sounds. In fact, most people find it very hard to articulate exactly what they would do with financial freedom.

Sooner or later, though, you'll need to answer the question. In fact, in Chapters 2 and 3, it will become a focal point. Meanwhile, let us show you how *our* answer to the question evolved. As you'll see, we didn't get it right, right away!

> *Capital as such is not evil; it is its wrong use that is evil.*
>
> —Indira Gandhi

Financial Freedom Strategy No. 2: Take Your First Freedom Step Today

We both always wanted to be millionaires. We clearly didn't inherit this desire, because our parents weren't rich, and—although they would have liked to have had more money—it was never a burning desire for them.

For us, it was. We wanted *freedom*.

We saw that the lack of money bothered our father/grandfather. He felt trapped in a business he didn't like, and he didn't know how to break out. He didn't have a money mentor. There was very little finance-related information or education available to people like him (particularly when you think about what is available today).

So what he and our mother/grandmother did was what they knew: work hard, send their children to college, and set aside money for retirement by making small investments in real estate. That was their plan, and they followed it.

We wanted *more*. Why? Because, as we saw it, money gives people freedom. With money, we thought, you can go where you want to go and do what you want to do, when you want to do it.

> *A wise leader rigorously adheres to method and discipline.*
>
> —George S. Patton

What we had to discover—and in fact didn't discover for many years—was that *having the money* wasn't as important as *knowing what to do with the money* once we got it. In reality, as it turned out, money was only a tool. In order to use that tool properly, we needed to first control our minds. We needed to aim our thoughts in a direction that had meaning and importance.

In fact, both of us had badly miscalculated in our early quests for financial freedom. With the benefit of hindsight, we can now see that not only do you have to plan for how you will achieve financial freedom, you also have to know how you will keep that freedom once you get it. With wealth comes responsibility—not only to yourself, but also to your family and others who mean the most to you.

Unfortunately, that lesson was a rather expensive one to learn. We sincerely hope that you won't have to learn it the hard way, as we did. (This is one important reason why we've written this book.) For now, suffice it to say that *making it* and *keeping it* are really two separate parts of the equation. If we can help you understand that, you're likely to make more and keep more.

To take your first step and set your mind on the course to financial success, you must begin to dream. You must begin to envision the kind of life you desire. For some

> *The price of greatness is responsibility.*
>
> —Winston Churchill

of you, this will be easy, because you have dreamed all your life. For others, it will be more difficult. Why? Some people simply don't know *how* to dream—they've never tapped into their imagination deeply enough to let their thoughts run free. Other people, deep down, don't believe that they *deserve* wealth or success.

But they're wrong. *Everyone* deserves a better place in life, and the dream has to come first. And if you've never let your imagination run free in this way, there's no time like the present.

Let's try a little exercise. Find a quiet place where there are no distractions. Think about your future financial freedom for just a moment. Envision the future—not just when you reach some arbitrary financial milestone, but further into the future. Think about your life *after* you achieve the financial freedom that you want.

What will you do with the money? Visualize yourself actually spending money on things you have always wanted. Would you buy a new car if you had a lot more money? Can you see yourself actually driving your old car into that showroom and buying that dream car?

Having trouble? This process of visualization may be very hard for some of you, mainly because for so many years, you have blocked out the possibility of great things happening to you. You assumed that if you didn't think too much about your financial worries, then that might make your frustrations a little easier to take. It's an "out of sight, out of mind" approach.

But that type of attitude is *precisely what you should move away from*. Dare to dream again! Get those creative juices flowing. Think back to the excitement that life held when you were a teenager, and everything seemed possible. (If you're a teenager now, congratulations for confronting these issues at such an early age; you're almost guaranteed success.) If at first you don't succeed in dreaming, try and try again.

If you achieved financial freedom, what would you buy for yourself? What would you buy for a member of your family? Can you see yourself spending your money, laughing, and having a good time? Giving a loved one something that he or she has always wanted? Good. You must start dreaming before this process can begin to work for you. Remember, mental rewards are just as good as physical ones.

> *The secret of success is constancy to purpose.*
> —Benjamin Disraeli

All right, we're willing to bet that at least some of you didn't go through that exercise. Well, we're going to stop right here and give you another chance. (If you did it, do it again.) *Pause* for a moment. No one's timing you. Let yourself go. (What's the downside? There is none!) Give your mind a chance to create the kind of future you've always wanted. Try it *now*.

Welcome back. Dreaming is fun, isn't it?

Once you have actually seen yourself spending and enjoying your newfound financial success, you can move on. Please don't fudge—we have a long way to go, and you simply can't do an end run around this first exercise.

OK, let's move on together. Let's change your visual focus. Where do you live in your new life of prosperity? What does your house look like? How many bedrooms does it have? Can you see it? If you can see it, spend a few minutes creating details. If you can't see it, spend a little more time with the exercise until you can.

Someone once said that what the mind can see, the body can achieve. We believe it. We go a step further. We believe that the mind *must* see it before the body is able to work for it.

Look at another realm of human endeavor: sports. When Roger Bannister broke the four-minute mile, he *saw* it long before he *did* it. Over and over in his mind, he later recalled, he visualized doing what had been deemed to be impossible. Interestingly enough, once Bannister did what no one else had ever done before, others quickly succeeded in doing it. Why? Because in minds all around the world, *mental barriers had been broken.* People understood that the impossible was now possible.

The same analogy applies to wealth creation. There is a process one must go through to achieve it. Bill Gates, in his best-selling book *The Road Ahead*, writes about his "play" with computers in high

> *The difficult we do immediately; the impossible takes a little longer.*
>
> —U.S. Army slogan

school. Even then, when computers were the size of large rooms and far less powerful than our miniature hand-held PDAs, he dreamed about what they would be able to achieve in the future.

His dream was so strong, in fact, that he feared missing out on the revolution he saw in his mind. He dropped out of Harvard University—dropped off the safe path he was on—to get a quicker start. There was simply no way that he was going to let the software revolution start without him.

Bill Gates saw the future of computers in his mind long before it became a reality. He saw a role for himself in that future. He dreamed the dream, developed plans to fulfill that dream, and then took action. This could be called the "science of success."

It's not restricted to Roger Bannister and Bill Gates. It's something that each of you can participate in and benefit from. But before you can do it, you have to knock down the mental barriers to your financial success. You must learn to envision your achievements. Once you do, the achievements will follow.

So far, so good? Are you beginning to see the mindset you need to have if you are to achieve financial freedom? Let's go a little further. What about a family? Will you have a spouse? Children? What will they be like? These are extremely important thoughts to consider and plan for. You must see it before it happens, but once you do, financial freedom will be more than one step closer.

All of the questions we have posed to you so far will become an important part of creating your dreams and ultimately achieving goals based on those dreams. Now that you see the process unfolding, you can also see how the end results will be different for everyone.

Each of us creates our own world, today and tomorrow, by the thoughts and dreams we create. This is precisely why financial freedom is viewed so differently once you get past the dollar number. Our dreams are all different, and that variety is a good thing. Can you imagine how difficult life would be if we all wanted to be doctors?

In order for life to work, we must all be different. We must have different dreams and different aspirations. But this very variety means that these dreams can all be fulfilled—assuming that each of us is honest with himself or herself and finds his or her *true* dream. Not someone else's dream—*your* dream.

Financial freedom is your dream. As long as you can dream, you can continue to succeed. Show us a person who has no dream, and we'll show you someone who is poor. A millionaire dreams, and then sets out to make those dreams real.

Once you stop dreaming, you stop the magic. That's because you have created the world you wanted. You stop moving forward, because your dreams have ended. Either you are content to live with what you

I like the dreams of the future better than the history of the past.

—Thomas Jefferson

have or you are constantly frustrated because you don't have enough—or you learn to dream again.

Think about this for a moment. Look around you at the people you know who, when measured in terms of financial prosperity, have a successful life. Inevitably, the ones who are the happiest are the ones who are still dreaming. Those who have stopped dreaming become overly concerned about the money they have. They begin to hoard their wealth in a way that restricts even their own pleasure. It's a sad predicament—to be snared by your failing or extinguished dreams.

As our mother/grandmother always said, "Be careful what you wish for, because you may get it." In other words, be ready to handle the consequences of what you think you want, because you may indeed get it. Money without a plan is worthless. That is why the first three chapters of this book are devoted to creating that plan. *You must be ready for your wealth before you get it.*

The plan you develop for financial success will be based on sound fundamentals, rather than on some pie-in-the-sky, get-rich-quick scheme. You *can* build the wealth you seek. It won't come overnight, but once you master our method, you won't care. You will be systematically working toward your long-term goal, while at the same time earning money and enjoying the journey. Isn't that what you *really* want? Satisfaction today, and financial freedom tomorrow?

To accomplish your goal of becoming financially free, you will need to master specific principles of wealth creation. No, these aren't some magical set of principles we found scratched in papyrus scrolls in the ruins of an ancient temple. They're contemporary, common-sense principles. At the same time, though, they *are* magical, because they create the basis for a sound foundation of wealth creation.

You need to be systematic and thorough in your approach to these principles. If you follow just some of them, you may still become financially free. (Yes, they are that powerful.) But your foundation for long-term success will be more solid if you internalize them all.

Let's take another short step in your journey toward financial freedom. Yes, we're going to do some more dreaming. If possible, you should find some quiet place where you can be by yourself and not have to worry about being self-conscious. But if you can't, don't worry about it. Just do the best you can. If you're not happy about the results the first time, consider repeating the exercise again later in a more private place, and see if the results are the same.

So get comfortable and relaxed. Close your eyes for a moment, and allow yourself to dream. Let your mind roam as if you were a little kid in school, bored by some dull assignment. Give yourself permission to do what people have told you not to do your entire life: *daydream*. Let your mind wander, and think happy thoughts—thoughts about things you would really like to do. Places where you've always wanted to travel. People you'd like to meet. Whatever comes to your mind, allow yourself to let go and dream, even if it is only for a few moments. Once you complete this brief exercise—and *only* after you have done this—continue on.

> *Large views always triumph over small ideas.*
> —Winston Churchill

Did you do it? Great. We hope you enjoyed this moment with yourself. It's a good start, and it's something you should do more often. At first, your conscious brain—the scolding part, the part that Freud called the "superego"—will resist your attempts at daydreaming. And let's face it, you're out of practice. You haven't done it since you were a kid, and even then, people were telling you it was a "waste of time."

Nothing could be further from the truth. Dreaming puts you in touch with your inner self. It allows you to contemplate what is going on in your life, and what you want to do about it. It is a restful time—a time that allows you to recharge your batteries and rejuvenate yourself, mentally, physically, and spiritually. Entire civilizations in the East endorse meditation as a positive habit to develop. We do, too—although we prefer to talk about dreaming, rather than meditating. We believe that a *focused* kind of meditation, a dreaming of your future, is critically important.

Financial Freedom Strategy No. 3: Focus Your Dreams to Make Them Come Alive

The next step in the process is to *focus your dream*. Pretend that, for once in your life, you had unlimited money and unlimited time. Don't necessarily go crazy with your thoughts, but work to eliminate those initial barriers of time and money. What will you be interested in *after* you buy all of those lavish things you always thought you wanted? What's beyond the bigger car, the faster boat, and the fancier house? Whatever they are, those are the really important things.

What 10 things would you do if you had unlimited time and money? Give yourself a few moments to come up with 10 answers, but not ones that are too long. Please write them down, either here or on a separate sheet of paper.

EXERCISE 2

1. _____
2. _____
3. _____
4. _____
5. _____
6. _____
7. _____
8. _____
9. _____
10. _____

Well, what did you find out about yourself? One thing many people discover, as a result of this exercise, is that listing 10 items is not as easy as they assumed it would be—even with unlimited time and money.

If you found that to be true—if numbers 9 and 10 came hard—then you need to dream more. Have at it! You are now free to dream.

YOUR MISSION TO WEALTH TO-DO LIST

1. DEVISE A PLAN FIRST, AND THE STRATEGIES WILL
   FOLLOW. You must come up with your plan first.
   Hildebrant's principle applies here: "If you don't
   know where you're going, any road will get you there."
   Wandering aimlessly will get you nowhere fast.

2. **TRUST YOUR MENTORS.** To get the most out of this book (or any other financial guide), you must put your trust in people you don't know. So we ask you to suspend disbelief. We ask you to think of the authors as people you know and trust as you progress through this book. (There's no downside and plenty of upside.)

3. **CHANGE YOUR MINDSET.** Accumulating wealth is as much about mindset as it is about net worth. It may sound simple or even naive, but without the proper mindset, you almost certainly will not achieve your financial goals. If you *do* somehow achieve them, they're likely to come undone quickly.

4. **DARE TO DREAM.** Dreaming is one of the first steps on the journey to financial independence. Think of Roger Bannister's four-minute mile. Think of John F. Kennedy's challenge to Americans to *get to the moon before the end of the decade.* You must first envision the future before it can become a reality. That may sound like an oversimplification (and indeed, it's only part of the story), but that's exactly what worked for us.

★ ★ ★

CHAPTER 2

Discover Your Dreams, Goals, and Values

*If you get the objectives right, even a
lieutenant can write the strategy.*

—Donald Rumsfeld

Allowing yourself to dream is the first step toward financial success. Now you must build upon that cornerstone to turn those dreams into reality. To do so will require that you set specific goals based upon the dreams you wrote down in Chapter 1.

ALIGN YOUR DREAMS, GOALS, AND VALUES FOR LASTING SUCCESS

In the many training sessions we have hosted over the years, we have noticed that many people have a difficult time with goal setting. They understand intellectually the value of setting goals, but they can't see how it applies to their own lives. In almost all cases, we've also noticed, these people lack the two prerequisites for setting goals: understanding the concept of goals and relating that concept to their own lives.

Maybe this sounds self-evident, but we'll say it anyway: Before you can set a goal, you have to understand what a goal is. Simply put, a goal is a *dream fixed to a certain time*. The dream is something you desire. The time element affixes it to your personal world and your reality. The dream is no longer simply floating in space; now it has a real "time meaning" attached to it, and it must be dealt with.

Second, the goal must relate to a personal value. Goals are the answer to the question, *What is important to you in life?* Values are the answer to why you want to accomplish those goals. If you don't relate your goal to your values, that goal will remain as lost—floating in space—as it was before you attached it to the reality of time.

This is one reason why you can't simply adopt someone else's goals for your life. The chances that you'll share that person's deepest values are incredibly small. Therefore, a goal that makes sense for him or her is likely to make little sense for you.

> *I have found the best way to give advice to your children is to find out what they want and then advise them to do it.*
>
> —Harry S. Truman

It is also why it is foolish for parents to push their children onto a particular career path, or—worse—into accomplishing something that they had not been able to achieve for themselves. Why? Because the goal that is being set for the child is based on the *parents'* dream rather than the child's. Yes, you can help someone nurture her or his own dreams, but you can't dream *for* someone else. The most rewarding thing a parent can do for a child is help that child discover his or her own dreams and learn how to fulfill them.

SHAPE YOUR DREAMS

Becoming a millionaire is a feasible goal, but depending on where you start financially, the journey can be long. You will need strength of purpose to stay on course. Without that mental strength, it becomes too easy to have both your attention and your money diverted. Neither can be allowed to happen if you want to stay on the path to financial freedom.

In order to reach your goal, you must first learn to *define it specifically*. If you are unsure of your objective, it will be easy for you to become distracted. For example, if you start only with the general desire to "make more money," you may well achieve that goal—but chances are you won't *keep* the money.

I conceive that the greatest part of the miseries of mankind are brought upon them by false estimates they have made of the value of things.

—Benjamin Franklin

You'll soon discover that there is no end to the amount you can spend if you don't relate it to certain standards. The 2,500-square-foot house will become a 3,500-square-foot house. The 3,500-square-foot house will become the 5,000-square-foot house. The "first new car" will evolve into the "first luxury car," which will evolve into the "top of the line new car traded in every two years."

Because you have no specific plan, you will be trapped on the up escalator. You will spend more and more, because you will think that the very acquisition of things will make you happy. Yes, you will find yourself in new, more luxurious surroundings—but instead of worrying about how you are going to make your $700-per-month house payment, you'll be worrying about how you will make the $4,000-per-month house payment.

You achieved your vague goal—*more money*—but somehow things got worse. The topic of worry (lack of money) has stayed the same, but now the practical burden you bear has become far heavier. You had a certain number of options to find replacement cash flow for the $700-per-month payment on your smaller home. But now that your payments are $4,000 per month, the options available to you for producing that much money are far fewer.

To stay off the up escalator—to avoid the "more money" treadmill—you need to decide what you do want, and in very precise terms. You need to *shape your dreams* by attaching them to time frames and specifics. At the same time, you need to make sure that the goals you set are aligned with your values.

Why? Because your values are the focal point of your internal happiness. If you set and achieve a goal that is in conflict with your values, not only will you be unhappy about having obtained that goal, but the result will have a negative influence on your desire to set and achieve *other* goals. Psychologically, you will begin to regard goal setting as an unhappy experience, even though that wasn't the problem in the first place. The *real* problem was that you didn't align the goals with your values.

> *It's the age-old struggle— the roar of the crowd on one side and the voice of your conscience on the other.*
>
> —Douglas MacArthur

We have some very good friends who worked for years to build a large company out of an idea they came up with together. They longed for the day when they could buy a huge house on the water in a very exclusive area of our town.

Because of their diligence and hard work, the company prospered, and they achieved their goal of purchasing their dream home. Unfortunately, the achievement of that goal didn't make them happy. Why not? Because that purchase separated them from their friends and their church, both of which—as it turned out— were things that they valued far more than that new house on the water.

And just to make things worse, they began to feel guilty about their newfound wealth. They worried that people might think they were showing off—even though that had never been their intent— and that people might become less friendly toward them. And in fact, their friends *did* begin to associate with them less frequently—in part because of their own feelings of jealousy and insecurity, and in part because their old friends now seemed *different* in their fancy new house. They seemed guarded and defensive rather than open and friendly.

While this couple came to understand the causes of what had happened, it didn't make them feel any better. The mistake they made was *not* in buying a big house on the water. (There's nothing inherently wrong with that goal.) The mistake they made was that they had defined and achieved a goal that didn't match their values.

How do you keep your goals and values aligned? That's the substance of the rest of this chapter. We have summarized the process in a series of seven steps:

Keep your eyes on the stars, but remember to keep your feet on the ground.

—Theodore Roosevelt

1. Create a list of goals and values.
2. Prioritize your goals.
3. Establish a plan to achieve your goals.
4. Take action on your goals.
5. Create success habits.
6. Rebalance your key objectives.
7. Enjoy, actualize, and repeat the process.

Goal-Setting Strategy No. 1: Create a List of Goals and Values

Values are what you believe about yourself. Goals, on the other hand, are targets that should capture those values and—once achieved—reinforce those values. In the case of our friends who became isolated, their goal was a hollow one, because it took them away from their fundamental values of friends and church. The goal was clearly at odds with their values. Without an alignment between values and goals, there will be no satisfaction. In fact, the only possible outcome is *dis*satisfaction.

Discovering your own values is one of the most important things you can do. And yet, very few people have ever even considered their values. So now we want you to try another exercise for us. Sit down in a quiet room and write down five personal values that you consider important. Don't think too hard about it—just start writing what comes into your mind. They will come to you. If you put down more than five, that's fine. (You won't be graded!)

If you need help getting started, that's OK, too. Just glance at this list of values shared by many people. Remember that while lists of values may overlap (in other words, you may use the same words as someone else), the *order* of the words and the weight you place upon them make the lists very different.

A close relationship with your mate
A good relationship with your family
A meaning of life
A relationship with God
Being highly regarded
Control of your destiny
Fame

Friendships

Giving to others

Good health

Happiness

Influence

Living to old age

Peace of mind

Possessions

Power

Purpose to work

Respect

Retirement

Security

Sense of accomplishment

Travel

Wealth

EXERCISE 3

Your Value List

1. _____

2. _____

3. _____

4. _____

5. _____

Now that you have made your list, rank your values from more important to less important (even though every value on this list is important).

Look at the result. Did you get it right? Are you happy with this summary of your values? If so, congratulations, because coming up with this list may be *the most important thing you will ever do*. Why? Because it is truly your road map to happiness.

For example, let's assume that your number one value is a close relationship with God, and your number two value is a close relationship with your family. And let's also assume that at the present time, you are pursuing a career that pays well and earns you lots of kudos and recognition but requires you to spend a great deal of time away from your family.

God is truth, and don't ever forget it.

—George S. Patton

Well, if that job doesn't somehow help you to develop a closer relationship with God, you are likely to be one miserable human being—and chances are, you won't even know *why*. Most likely, you are working hard, banking a lot of money, and feeling mostly empty inside. Your values are your *essence*. If you hope to achieve a happy life, you have to live a life and aspire to a future that captures and expresses those values.

Assume for a moment that a certain individual (let's call her Jane) has the following values:

1. A close relationship with God
2. A close relationship with family
3. Peace of mind
4. Security
5. Good health

Conspicuously absent from Jane's list (especially in a book about becoming financially free) is anything about "making lots of money." True, you could make the case that goals 3 through 5 presuppose financial security. But the point is, "making money" didn't make Jane's list.

Can you see the importance of this discovery? If Jane spends all of her time trying to become a millionaire, she is almost *certain* to be a very unhappy millionaire (if, indeed, she ever gets there). For Jane to be successful *in her own eyes*, her goals must be aligned with her values. To sharpen the point, let's consider the following question: Which of the following goals, if achieved, would make Jane happier?

1. Making $1 million
2. Setting up a faith-based charitable foundation with an endowment of $1 million

See the difference? Putting $1 million in the bank would probably make Jane feel OK, up to a point. But wouldn't endowing a faith-based charitable foundation do a lot more to make Jane feel satisfied with her life?

Let's take this illustration a step further. What if you changed the second goal to read: "Setting up a faith-based charitable foundation with an endowment of $1 million, in which all of my family members could work together." Wow! Do you see what that would mean to Jane? The better she understands her values, the more likely it is that she can set the right goals, give herself a life's mission, and live her life with *passion*.

So here's our next exercise, which builds directly on the last one, as well as on Jane's example. Take a few minutes to review the values you've written down and ranked. Now write down five goals that, if achieved, would capture and reinforce those values. Use the "dreams list" that you created in Chapter 1 and anchor those dreams in reality by assigning specific time frames to them.

EXERCISE 4

Your Goals

1. _____

2. _____

3. _____

4. _____

5. _____

Goal-Setting Strategy No. 2: Prioritize Your Goals

Now that you have established a list of goals, rank them. Renumber them as you did your values list, lining them up in their order of importance to you. And although we don't want to complicate the assignment too much, we encourage you to think about making two such lists: one ranked in order of *importance*, and the second ranked in order of *urgency*. Which goal is of the greatest enduring importance to you, and which do you want (or need) to accomplish first?

For example, if one of your goals is to build a $2 million retirement nest egg and another is to put your kids through college five years from now, it doesn't make a great deal of sense to concentrate on your retirement plan when you have a much more urgent need—unless, of course, the retirement plan is of *far greater importance* to you. If the goals are of equal importance, then urgency takes over, and your priority quickly becomes the tuition bills.

> *Some men see things as they are and say why? I dream things that never were and say "Why not?"*
> —Robert F. Kennedy

Goal-Setting Strategy No. 3: Establish a Plan to Achieve Your Goals

You have your goal. It is your top priority. Now, what are you going to *do* about it?

When our children were younger and we went on trips by car, we would call the American Automobile Association—"Triple A"—and ask it to do a trip plan for us. In a couple of weeks, AAA would send back a nice bound series of maps that told us the best way to get to our destinations. If there was construction along the way, for example, AAA would either suggest detours or carefully mark the construction area and advise us that there was a bumpy road ahead.

Wouldn't it be nice if life were like that? You could set your goal, call up Triple A, and get a plan laid out for you. Unfortunately, life isn't quite that easy. But with the help of the simple concepts in this book, you can learn how to do the plan *yourself.* The key to reaching any financial goal is to *have a plan.* Surprisingly, it's not so important that you pick the *perfect* road or the *perfect* investment system. Instead, the important thing is to pick a specific plan and stick with it until you reach your destination.

How do you create a plan to achieve your goals? The same way that you create a plan for a trip. You write down the moves that you need to make, step by step, to get to your destination. Just as you follow a map from Triple A to get to a geographic destination, you follow a specific plan to get to a financial destination.

One does not plan and then try to make circumstances fit those plans. One tries to make plans fit the circumstances.

—George S. Patton

Goal-Setting Strategy No. 4: Take Action on Your Goals

Our father/grandfather always said, "A turtle never gets anywhere unless he sticks his neck out." He was right. Ultimately, we have to take *action*. Otherwise, all our values, goals, and plans aren't worth the paper we put them on.

But taking action proves difficult for a lot of people, because they are filled with anxieties and insecurities. *Did I put down the right goal? Is my plan a good one?* These doubts paralyze the worrier, just like a deer caught in headlights.

Nevertheless, you must take action on the plan you create. Think of it as something like scaling a cliff. If you had to climb a cliff for the first time, how would you do it? You'd start out *slow* and *easy*. You'd pace yourself, going up foot by vertical foot. You don't have to break any speed record or take any unnecessary risks. Well, it's the same with acting on a financial plan. You don't have to reach millionaire status overnight. Financial success is an endurance event—a marathon rather than a sprint. Take off slowly, build to a comfortable pace, and stride to the finish.

Build your goal around a problem, not the other way around.

—Anonymous

How do you get started? It's easy. Take a look at your goals list. Pick the one goal on your list that seems the easiest to accomplish and also has near-term importance. Let's say that you wrote down, "Make $10,000 more this year."

That's a good goal. It's near-term, and it's specific. So let's use it to take action. Below your goal, create a plan to achieve the goal by listing the specific action steps you'll take to get there:

Goal   Make $10,000 more this year
Plan   Increase salary by $3,000

Action Step 1   Ask for a raise.

a. Create a list of reasons I deserve a raise.

b. Make an appointment with my boss.

Action Step 2   Start a small business.

a. Research businesses of interest.

b. Pick a business in 60 days.

c. Start the business in 90 days.

If you are like a lot of people who have never properly learned the techniques of goal setting, this method is likely to come as a pleasant surprise. For the first time, not only do you *see* your goal, but you see specific action steps that you can take to achieve it.

While the goal may seem difficult, the action steps to achieve the goal are often much easier. You will discover that taking each step puts you closer and closer to your goal, which in turn makes the goal appear easier and more attainable the closer you get to it.

Goal-Setting Strategy No. 5: Create Success Habits

Sometimes, with the best of intentions, parents do their children a disservice. We mentioned one such disservice in Chapter 1: defining daydreaming as a bad thing. (It's not.) Here's another disservice: continuously linking the words *habit* and *bad*. For example:

Quit biting your nails. It's a bad habit.
Stop smoking. It's a bad habit.
Don't drink so much. It's a bad habit.

Have you ever heard anyone praised for developing a *good* habit? Not often, and yet, good habits are critically important. The tennis star's consistent stroke, which leads to victories on the court, is the result of a good habit. The student who studies consistently and makes top grades has developed good study habits. In fact, any repetitive pattern that brings success deserves to be recognized and applauded, and should be built into one's system of goals: *I will continue this action until it becomes a habit.*

Achieving the goal of financial freedom offers us many "habit opportunities." In fact, each of the principles in this book should be developed into a positive habit. For example, the theme of Chapter 4, "Pay Yourself First," is all about habits. (In this case, the habit in question is not a recent concept but appears in the Bible.)

> *Even when I had nothing to do, I always vaguely felt that I had no time to waste.*
>
> —Napoleon Bonaparte

In Chapter 4, we discuss the principle of setting aside 10 percent of your income on a consistent basis and how this will provide for a comfortable future. A good habit, right? But few people actually *do* it, because establishing good habits takes work.

Other vital habits can be developed to help you maintain your success. Diversifying your portfolio, setting limits on losses, resisting the temptation to get greedy—all are proven investment rules that build both protection and consistency into your investment plan. If you take the time and effort to transform these rules into habits, you will profit substantially from the improved performance of your portfolio and the added protection they give you.

Goal-Setting Strategy No. 6: Rebalance Your Key Objectives

We hope that, by now, we have impressed upon you the importance of values and goals when it comes to your financial life. You should also understand that while some values may be consistent through-out your life, others may change. When they do, both your goals and your plans to reach those goals need to be reevaluated and rebalanced, in order to get your new value/goal structure into alignment. If you don't rebalance, it will be like deciding to stay on the road to New York after you've decided to go to San Francisco instead. Yes, you're still moving along a path, but you're sure to arrive at the wrong place.

To help you spot these changes as they occur in your life, we suggest that you set a particular time each year to rebalance your objectives. We have found the two weeks after Christmas to be a perfect time for this activity. Business always slows down during that time of year, and the decrease in activity gives you an opportunity to reflect.

Note the *consistency* in this approach. By consistently rebalancing our objectives at the same time each year, we have made this activity into a habit. While that time might not be good for you, pick one that is, rebalance your objectives, and (if necessary) refocus your life.

Goal-Setting Strategy No. 7: Enjoy, Actualize, and Repeat the Process

If you incorporate the six strategies, or steps, just outlined into your life, you will find a new sense of gratification and enjoyment. Now that your life is in alignment with who you are, you should begin to feel that you are headed in the right direction—much like the driver with the Triple A road maps. Take the time to *enjoy* this newfound sense of satisfaction.

At the same time, be prepared for that sense of satisfaction to ebb and even disappear. Just as the wheels on your car lose their alignment over time (and far more quickly if you hit a curb!), our lives also get "out of alignment" because of life's curbs. It is just a part of human nature: We get caught up in all sorts of things that we never intended to get caught up in.

What's important, though, is simply to understand that we must (1) enjoy things when they go well, (2) understand that misalignment will happen, and (3) get realigned when we hit that curb (or when life's twists and turns gradually lead to misalignment).

By repeating this process, you will enjoy your life more and continually refocus yourself on the things that are truly important to you. Once you are properly focused, it is easier to let go of those miscues that don't fit into your grand plan.

YOUR MISSION TO WEALTH TO-DO LIST

1. **UNDERSTAND THAT THE FIRST STEP TO FINANCIAL FREEDOM IS A GOAL.** Remember that a goal is what turns a dream into a reality. Without goals, there can be no "freedom" from anything, because you have not yet figured out what it is that you want.

2. **MAKE SURE THAT THERE IS ALIGNMENT BETWEEN YOUR GOALS AND YOUR VALUES.** Your values have to guide you as you make financial and other important life decisions. Without harmony between your goals and your values, you will almost certainly end up in the wrong place.

3. STUDY AND IMPLEMENT THE SEVEN STEPS OF ALIGNING GOALS AND VALUES.

1. Create a list of goals and values.

2. Prioritize your goals.

3. Establish a plan to achieve your goals.

4. Take action on your goals.

5. Create success habits.

6. Rebalance your key objectives.

7. Enjoy, actualize, and repeat the process.

★ ★ ★

CHAPTER 3

Discover Your Mission

He who is able to conquer others is powerful;
he who is able to conquer himself is more
powerful.

—Lao-tzu

You've gone through the exercises in the first two chapters of this book. As a result, you've dreamed new dreams, discovered new values, set goals for your future, and even created a plan to get there. Maybe, as a result of having taken these steps, you've started to discover a new sense of *clarity* in your life. Maybe you're beginning to feel that there is a reason for you to have these dreams, values, and goals.

Well, if so, you're right. There is a reason.

We believe that everyone on earth is here for a purpose, and that you are given a lifetime to serve that particular purpose. How long a period of time that represents is more or less irrelevant; it will be enough.

"How can that be?" you may well ask. "What about a child who lives for only a few years? Did she have a purpose?"

We still think the answer is yes. It's certainly true that the purpose of a life—especially a far shortened life—remains obscure to us mere mortals. Perhaps the tragedy of a dead child serves to demonstrate the value of life. (This is something that we sometimes understand only when it is taken away from us.) Perhaps someone affected by that tragedy behaves differently as a result of her bereavement and changes the world for the better. Sometimes the only thing we can say is, "This is not for us to understand."

Can someone who is afflicted with a chronic, debilitating disease have a purpose? Again, yes—absolutely. There is great value to be gained from enduring such a hardship. Ask anyone who has ever suffered through a prolonged illness. Such people aren't necessarily overjoyed about their experience, but they're very likely to acknowledge that they've gained a certain kind of wisdom as a result of it. They're also likely to express their gratitude for having achieved this kind of wisdom, even by a very difficult and unanticipated path.

Think about Christopher Reeve, the actor who was injured in a horse-riding accident and who recently passed away. Certainly, when he was playing Superman in the movies, he had no notion that his ultimate mission in life would be to hasten the development of better treatments for spinal-cord injuries. He certainly would never have *chosen* to become a quadriplegic. And yet, after his injury, he struggled heroically to live his life in as normal a way as possible—and to bring pressure to bear on the politicians and the medical community to find new therapies. And by so doing, he became a source of inspiration to millions.

We all have a mission to perform. Sometimes that mission becomes clear early in one's life, and the challenge is mainly one of staying on track and not getting distracted by the obstacles and challenges of everyday life. Sometimes that mission becomes clear (or changes abruptly) only when one's life takes a sudden turn in an unexpected direction, like Christopher Reeve's. Sometimes we embrace a mission that someone

Some men can live up to the loftiest ideals without ever going higher than a basement.

—Theodore Roosevelt

else has defined for us. In that case, we spend many years pursuing someone else's dream—all too often, a dream from which we wake up too late.

We believe that you can lead a life of joy only when you discover your mission and pursue it *energetically* and *successfully*. In part, it's about "going with the flow"—learning to play the cards that life deals you, whether at birth or at some subsequent point. Going against your own grain is silly.

For example, until well into the twentieth century, schoolteachers used to try to get left-handed children to write with their right hands. For those kids, learning to write with the wrong hand was frustrating, unnatural, and limiting. You need to discover and accept your own natural talents and inclinations, and to work with those talents and inclinations. The sooner you do so, the more productive you'll be and the more enjoyment you will get out of life.

And the faster you will progress down the path to financial freedom.

Mission Strategy No. 1: Discover Your Mission in Life

As you know, the title of this book is *Operation Financial Freedom*. So yes, we're talking about building and keeping wealth. But at the outset, we told you that we wanted to talk about more than just attaining riches. We also want to talk about discovering your mission and giving real value to the money you want to make. Why? Because we believe that financial freedom is about far more than economics. It's about how you see yourself in the world, how you view your wealth, and how you use that wealth to bring joy into people's lives—your own and others'.

> *The only realization of tomorrow will be our doubts of today, so let us move forward with strong and active faith.*
> —Franklin Delano Roosevelt

In previous chapters, we've helped you discover your financial freedom mindset, and also your goals and values. In this chapter, we conclude the first major part of the book, "Preparing for Your Mission to Wealth," by helping you pull your dreams, goals, and values into an all-encompassing mission statement.

Mission statements are commonly associated with large corporations and nonprofit institutions, not with individuals. These big institutions use their mission statements to build consensus internally and to present a clear and understandable face to the world.

We're going to use this tool on the *individual* level. Why? Because if we and you do our respective jobs right, this statement will become the focal point of everything you do. It will become a yardstick against which you can measure life's surprises and opportunities. It will provide a quick reality test to help you decide whether a particular turn of events is important or unimportant.

Developing a mission statement may seem like a monumental task. (Corporations sometimes spend many months, and involve lots of smart people, in the writing of *their* mission statements.) The prospect of sitting down and writing out a concise summary of your life's plan may boggle your imagination. But as with most difficult tasks, the secret lies in breaking down the monumental challenge into smaller, doable parts. Just as we have broken down the analysis of dreams, goals, and values in previous chapters, here we're going to break down the creation of a mission statement into bite-sized, accomplishable parts.

For example, although mission statements can vary dramatically in length, most of them consist of three basic building blocks. Each of these building blocks can be phrased as a question, as follows:

1. What action word describes what you intend to do?
2. What is your core value?
3. Whom do you intend to affect?

Obviously, every organization answers these questions differently. Maybe an example or two would help to underscore both those differences and the underlying building-block similarities. Here's a short and sweet one from Microsoft:

> *At Microsoft, we work to help people and businesses throughout the world realize their full potential. This is our mission. Everything we do reflects this mission and the values that make it possible.*

The American Cancer Society's mission statement is only a little bit longer:

> *The American Cancer Society is the nationwide community-based voluntary health organization dedicated to eliminating cancer as a major health problem by preventing cancer, saving lives, and diminishing suffering from cancer, through research, education, advocacy, and service.*

Up along the Hudson, West Point emphasizes its impact on its cadets:

To educate, train, and inspire the Corps of Cadets so that each graduate is a commissioned leader of character committed to the values of Duty, Honor, Country; professional growth throughout a career as an officer in the United States Army; and a lifetime of selfless service to the nation.

And from another corner of academia, it may not surprise you to learn that Harvard College's mission statement is a lot longer:

Harvard College adheres to the purposes for which the Charter of 1650 was granted: "The advancement of all good literature, arts, and sciences; the advancement and education of youth in all manner of good literature, arts, and sciences; and all other necessary provisions that may conduce to the education of the . . . youth of this country. . . ." In brief: Harvard strives to create knowledge, to open the minds of students to that knowledge, and to enable students to take best advantage of their educational opportunities.

To these ends, the College encourages students to respect ideas and their free expression, and to rejoice in discovery and in critical thought; to pursue excellence in a spirit of productive cooperation; and to assume responsibility for the consequences of personal actions. Harvard seeks to identify and to remove restraints on students' full participation, so that indi-

viduals may explore their capabilities and interests and may develop their full intellectual and human potential. Education at Harvard should liberate students to explore, to create, to challenge, and to lead. The support the College provides to students is a foundation upon which self-reliance and habits of lifelong learning are built: Harvard expects that the scholarship and collegiality it fosters in its students will lead them in their later lives to advance knowledge, to promote understanding, and to serve society.

All these mission statements are pretty different—and yet, they are also pretty similar in their effect on the reader. You walk away from each of these statements with a pretty good sense of what each of these institutions is all about. That's what this chapter intends to do for you, as an individual.

Let's look at the three building blocks, beginning with the action question: *What do you intend to do?*

> *Plan backwards as well as forward. Set objectives and trace back to see how to achieve them.*
>
> —Donald Rumsfeld

Mission Strategy No. 2: Find What You Want to Do

Think in terms of action words that have meaning to you. For example, in our lives, the word *teach* has great meaning. Almost everything we do that brings us great joy centers on teaching. Sometimes that is by writing and sometimes by speaking. Sometimes we are teaching a large group; at other times, we are focused on one of our children. In any event, the action that brings our greatest motivation is teaching.

The ablest man I ever met is the man you think you are.

—Franklin Delano Roosevelt

What action words fit you? Perhaps one or more immediately come to mind. If they don't, use the following list to help you. As with all of the exercises so far, we strongly suggest that you *take the time to do it now.* You are missing the point—and delaying your progress on the path to financial freedom—if you don't.

ACTION WORDS

Teach	Speak
Preach	Motivate
Build	Sell
Accomplish	Write
Affirm	Team
Communicate	Provide
Create	Lead
Realize	Make
Master	Persuade

After you have thought about what you like or want to do, write down the word that best describes it. If you can define it more specifically, you can add subcategories, but that's not a must.

If you feel that more than one action word is required to really capture your desire, feel free. Use as many as you need. After all, this is *your* mission statement, not ours, and there are no right or wrong answers.

Now, use that word (or those words) in a sentence like the one in the following exercise.

EXERCISE 5

Example:
My mission is to *teach.*

Or:
My mission is to *teach* by *writing* and *speaking.*

Now it's your turn. Please complete the blank.
My mission is to _____

Great! You did it. Whatever you wrote down, if you "own" it, *it's a powerful statement.* And, believe it or not, through the simple act of thinking about it and writing it down, you've moved much further toward reaching your dreams than the vast majority of people you'll ever meet.

> *History will be kind to me for I intend to write it.*
>
> —Winston Churchill

Mission Strategy No. 3: Determine Your Core Values

The second part of your mission statement relates to your core values. In the last chapter, you made a list of those values. It's now time to put them to use. If for some reason you didn't select the values that had the greatest influence on your life, let's do it now. The following list gives examples to help jog your mind when you think about your values.

VALUES

Happiness

Peace of mind

Security

Good health

Wealth

A relationship with God

A close relationship with your mate

A good relationship with your family

Purpose to work

A meaning of life

Fame

Friendships

Power

Control of your destiny

Living to old age

Sense of accomplishment

Influence

Respect

Being highly regarded

Possessions

Travel

Retirement

Giving to others

EXERCISE 6

Write down the one or two things you value most:

1. _____

_____

2. _____

_____

Mission Strategy No. 4: Target the People You Intend to Affect

The final part of your mission statement answers the question of the person, people, or groups you are trying to reach. Perhaps it's your children. Perhaps it's *all* children. Maybe it's women, men, or a particular segment of the population, such as battered women or teenage runaways. Whatever the group, it should be the one that motivates you the most. You've felt this instinct before. Now it's time to *commit*. The more passion you feel, the greater your mission will become. Identify the cause or group that you are most interested in reaching. You will need the answer for Exercise 7.

Mission Strategy No. 5: Write Your Mission Statement

You are now about to do what few people have actually done: Put all three parts together and create your own personal mission statement.

EXERCISE 7

My mission in life is to _____

                                                   Action Word   What

to _____ .

                        Who

Finished? Congratulations! Again, this is a wonderful accomplishment. It would be nice if we could promise you that this is the only mission statement you'll ever have to write. But most likely, that's not true. Most likely, the statement you just completed will change as you learn more about yourself in the years ahead. But that's OK too, because it reflects the learning and growing that come with a rich and satisfying life.

> *Never tell people how to do things. Tell them what to do and they will surprise you with their ingenuity.*
>
> —George S. Patton

When you first opened this book, your only goal was to become financially free. Now you know much more. You know *why* you want to achieve that goal, and *what you will do* when you achieve financial freedom.

It is also worth mentioning that by now you may have discovered that money isn't one of the things that's most important to you. Is that a useful discovery? We think it is. Because now you are totally free to work on *your* true mission in life, rather than on what somebody else decided was important for you. This can only help make you *more* successful. It's like being your own boss, psychologically.

Now take one final step for us. Share your mission with someone you love who is likely to be supportive of your plan. Tell that person what it means to you. Why? Because sharing your mission can help you bring it to life. It's no longer just an idea floating in your head. Now it's something that has been declared to the world, a little bit like a marriage vow. Enjoy the moment, and recognize that it is precious. *You are embarking on a journey like none you've ever taken before.*

YOUR MISSION TO WEALTH TO-DO LIST

1. DISCOVER YOUR MISSION. It will be different for everyone. The key is to identify exactly what it is that you want out of life, and then to set the right goals to achieve it.

2. UNDERSTAND YOUR OWN HISTORY. Heed the advice of Winston Churchill by writing your own history. For you, this means deciding for yourself the things that will be most important to you, and then striving to make them real.

3. CONSTRUCT YOUR OWN MISSION STATEMENT. Using the tools provided earlier (action words, the things you most value, and the group that is most important to you), put on paper your own mission statement. (Please do not go on to the next chapter without completing this vital step.) Then share it with someone who understands you and is likely to understand what it means to you. Don't be shy about this. The right person in your life will feel honored to be asked. Trust us on this one.

★ ★ ★

PART 2

Mission Critical

I n Part 2 of this book, we zero in on those habits, tactics, and strategies that will place you firmly on your path to wealth. For example, we start with one of the fundamental, inescapable, critical rules of wealth creation: *pay yourself first.* Few principles of wealth creation are more important than making sure you set aside a certain sum of money for your future *before* you start to spend.

We will show you how to "save your way to wealth" and how to establish and build good credit (or rebuild your credit profile, if necessary). We will show you the best way to buy high-ticket items like cars without breaking the bank.

And we will wrap up this "mission critical" part of the book by explaining why owning your own home is—and always will be—one of the most important things that you can do to secure your financial future.

★ ★ ★

CHAPTER 4

Pay Yourself First

It is better to have an ambitious plan than none at all.

—Winston Churchill

F ear plays a specific (but different) role in each of our lives. Of course, some of us are more affected than others. But at least to a certain degree, almost all of us experience some measure of fear for our own well-being. As fear relates to money, it is often a motivating force for people's individual desire to accumulate. The need is not so much for what the money can do now as it is to protect us from unknown forces down the road.

Some people don't seem to have this instinct at all, and this doesn't bode well for the long-term health of the American economy. (We have the lowest savings rate of any developed nation, which is a worrisome thing.) But the rest of us experience this self-protec-

There is no security on this earth; there is only opportunity.

—Douglas MacArthur

tive instinct to put something aside for a rainy day. For some people, this means setting aside a small amount of money for less fortunate times. For still another group, the fear becomes extreme—even irrational—and leads to the unnecessary hoarding (and often *counting*) of money.

Saving Strategy No. 1: Determine How Much Is Enough

Let's acknowledge first that *saving money for the future is important*. Having said that, the inevitable question that follows is, How much is enough? Setting aside a little money isn't difficult, but since small amounts can seem so insignificant, it's easy to lose the discipline to continue. But it is that very discipline that makes saving work. Well, discipline combined with the almost magical power of compound interest.

Discipline must be a habit so engrained that it is stronger than the excitement of battle or the fear of death.

—George S. Patton

Compound interest is the key to building wealth. Simply put, it means investing some money, earning interest on your investment, and then leaving both the interest and the principal in place so that you begin to earn interest on your interest (as well as on your principal).

In other words, first your original money earns money, and then the money your money has earned earns more money. This goes on year after year. After years of compounded growth, the annual earnings reach an acceptable level. Eventually, if your original investment was large enough, if your rates of interest were competitive, and if you wait long enough, your nest egg will grow large enough to produce an acceptable outside income.

To answer the proverbial question of how much money is enough money, we have created a hypothetical example. What would happen to an individual's savings for retirement if that individual did nothing more than save 10 percent of her or his gross earnings, invested the money in the stock market, and left it until age 65? Let's work through this hypothetical example.

Let's assume that this individual, a young woman, starts working at age 22 and receives a 3 percent cost-of-living raise each year. Also assume she receives four merit increases: two for $5,000 each, and two for $10,000 each. These increases are allowed for advancement and special job promotions or changes. Certainly, these increases are not guaranteed, but they are not unreasonable; in fact, they're reasonable over a lifetime of work.

Now let's add a few more assumptions. Assume that after age 47, she gets no additional raises or increases in salary. Finally, assume that she does nothing more than take 10 percent of everything she makes and "pays herself first." The money was set aside for special situations and retirement. She invests all her savings in the stock market, which, history tells us, will produce an annual return of about 12 percent over an individual's lifetime. This approximately matches the historical return of the Dow Jones Industrial Average over the past 20 years (11.5 percent, in fact).

Again, our subject is a young woman who is initially making $27,000 per year. For ease of calculation, we'll assume that she makes the full contribution of 10 percent of her gross annual salary at the beginning of the year. At the end of the first year, therefore, her 10 percent contribution of $2,700 is now worth $3,024, based on a 12 percent return.

At the end of the second year, we add the previous year's ending balance ($3,024) and the new year's 10 percent contribution ($2,781, which includes a 3 percent raise), then multiply the total by 1.12 to show her compounded return at a 12 percent rate. The table below illustrates how her money grows.

FORTY-THREE YEARS OF GROWTH

AGE	SALARY (3% Annual Increase)	YEARLY $ CONTRIBUTION (10% of Salary)	ENDING BALANCE*
22	$27,000.00	$2,700.00	$3,024.00
23	$27,810.00	$2,781.00	$6,501.60
24	$28,644.30	$2,864.43	$10,489.95
25	$29,503.63	$2,950.36	$15,053.15
26	$30,388.74	$3,038.87	$20,263.07
27	$31,300.40	$3,130.04	$26,200.29
28	$36,300.40 ($5,000 increase)	$3,630.04	$33,409.96
29	$37,389.41	$3,738.94	$41,606.77
30	$38,511.09	$3,851.11	$50,912.83
31	$39,666.43	$3,966.64	$61,465.01
32	$40,856.42	$4,085.64	$73,416.73
33	$42,082.11	$4,208.21	$86,939.93
34	$47,082.11 ($5,000 increase)	$4,708.21	$102,645.92
35	$48,494.57	$4,849.46	$120,394.82
36	$49,949.41	$4,994.94	$140,436.54

AGE	SALARY (3% Annual Increase)	YEARLY $ CONTRIBUTION (10% of Salary)	ENDING BALANCE*
37	$51,447.89	$5,144.79	$163,051.09
38	$52,991.33	$5,299.13	$188,552.24
39	$54,581.07	$5,458.11	$217,291.59
40	$64,581.07 ($10,000 increase)	$6,458.11	$250,599.66
41	$66,518.50	$6,651.85	$288,121.70
42	$68,514.06	$6,851.41	$330,369.87
43	$70,569.48	$7,056.95	$377,918.04
44	$72,686.56	$7,268.66	$431,409.10
45	$74,867.16	$7,486.72	$491,563.31
46	$84,867.16 ($10,000 increase)	$8,486.72	$560,056.03
47	$85,000.00 (Salary caps out)	$8,500.00	$636,782.76
48	$85,000.00	$8,500.00	$722,716.69
49	$85,000.00	$8,500.00	$818,962.69
50	$85,000.00	$8,500.00	$926,758.22
51	$85,000.00	$8,500.00	$1,047,489.20
52	$85,000.00	$8,500.00	$1,182,707.91
53	$85,000.00	$8,500.00	$1,334,152.85
54	$85,000.00	$8,500.00	$1,503,771.20
55	$85,000.00	$8,500.00	$1,693,743.74
56	$85,000.00	$8,500.00	$1,906,512.99
57	$85,000.00	$8,500.00	$2,144,814.55
58	$85,000.00	$8,500.00	$2,411,712.29

(Cont.)

AGE	SALARY (3% Annual Increase)	YEARLY $ CONTRIBUTION (10% of Salary)	ENDING BALANCE*
59	$85,000.00	$8,500.00	$2,710,637.77
60	$85,000.00	$8,500.00	$3,045,434.30
61	$85,000.00	$8,500.00	$3,420,406.42
62	$85,000.00	$8,500.00	$3,840,375.19
63	$85,000.00	$8,500.00	$4,310,740.21
64	$85,000.00	$8,500.00	$4,837,549.04
65	$85,000.00	$8,500.00	$5,427,574.92

*Ending balance is last year's ending balance, plus this year's dollar contribution, times 1.12.

The conclusion from this example is clear. By the age of 65, this individual will have amassed a nest egg of more than $5.4 million! True, the example is grossly oversimplified. We have not deducted any amount for taxes, for example, although that amount would be minimized by maximum usage of 401(k)s, IRAs, and other deductible retirement plan contributions. We have also not factored in the decreased buying power resulting from the effects of inflation.

On the other hand, we didn't discuss the effects of combining income with a spouse, an added inheritance at some point, or any other positive contribution.

What you have before you is simply an example. We want you to clearly see that long-term savings build wealth. We also want you to see that because of compounding, the sooner you start, the better. Finally, we hope you see that building a nest egg for your future doesn't take as much money as you

Never leave that till tomorrow which you can do today.

—Benjamin Franklin

may have been led to believe. The key is to start early, be persistent in the middle, and allow yourself to enjoy some of the fruits of your labor along the way.

Savings Strategy No. 2: Create a System to Set Aside Money

How do you accomplish this savings task? We've already told you: *Pay yourself first.* This means creating a personal system that sets aside money from your current income for your long-term nest egg. In Chapter 2, we discussed the importance of building success habits that we call "automatics": our method of creating successful systems that you do without thought.

Paying yourself first is an example of a successful "automatic" that will create the long-term result you want. In this case, set aside 10 percent of your gross income each month for the long term. As you can see from our example, for most people, *this will be enough*, and you won't have to worry about your future retirement.

If you don't think the numbers in our example apply to your situation, adjust it as you see fit. The point is to create a system to get there, and then put it to work at the earliest possible moment in time.

Once you determine the amount you want to set aside consistently, make it automatic, so that you aren't tempted to stray each month. Even if you can't start with 10 per-

> *Innovation of course involves experiment.*
> —Winston Churchill

cent, set aside at least *some* consistent percentage of what you make in order to develop the automatic habit. Use a payroll deduction or set up an automatic debit from your checking account each month to go into your investing account.

Once your money goes into your investing account, it will automatically be invested according to your "incremental investing program," discussed in detail in Chapter 11.

Having established an automatic savings and investment program, you are now free to enjoy life—which was one of the major purposes of this book in the first place.

YOUR MISSION TO WEALTH TO-DO LIST

1. **STUDY THE MAGIC OF COMPOUND INTEREST.** In 1783, publisher and investor Ben Franklin left gifts of $5,000 each to the cities of Boston and Philadelphia, saying that they could take out $500,000 after 100 years (for public works), and then would get access to the rest after another hundred years. In 1991, each of those accounts was worth more than $20 million.

2. **PUT THE MAGIC OF COMPOUND INTEREST TO WORK.** Set aside a predetermined amount each month. You may want to work with an accountant, a financial advisor, the payroll manager at work, or some other professional to figure out exactly how much will come out of your *net* income if you set aside (for example) 10 percent of your *gross*. Assuming that you put the money in tax-deferred accounts like IRAs or 401(k)s, the "real" reduction in your net will be substantially less than 10 percent. Once you know the amount, you can get started. However, the number should be a percentage of your salary. As your salary increases, your savings dollar amount will increase with it.

3. **STICK TO IT.** The money that you put aside in Year 1 will begin working its compound-interest magic. But to get that really big nest egg in place, you'll have to contribute to your accounts faithfully, year after year. This is less painful than it sounds, if you never give yourself access to the money in the first place. It wasn't ever in your monthly budget, so you didn't get used to having it to spend.

4. **RESIST TEMPTATION.** Federal tax codes have made it easier to take money out of (or borrow against) your retirement accounts for various good causes: education, health emergencies, home purchases, and so on. Resist the temptation. If you take that money out, you're unlikely to ever put it back.

★ ★ ★

CHAPTER 5

Save Your Way to Wealth

The process of the creation of new wealth is beneficial to the whole community.

—Winston Churchill

As you begin to focus on your goal of financial freedom, you will want to have money to invest in order to build long-term wealth. There are essentially two ways to generate more money for yourself: You can make more, or you can spend less. Pretty amazing, right? It all boils down to that.

Here's another potential surprise: In a lot of cases, it's actually easier and more "profitable" to get money by spending less than it is to always worry about making more. Why? Because when you make more, you pay 25 to 35 percent in taxes on that extra income. If you generate money by spending less, 100 percent of that savings will immediately drop down to your bottom line.

Spending less *doesn't* mean that you have to pinch pennies to the point of taking all the fun out of life. That mistaken notion is what drives people away from saving in the first place. In fact, you need to control your spending only to the point of ensuring that you can pay yourself the first 10 percent (as we discussed in the previous chapter) and still meet your other obligations. The alternatives aren't very attractive. If you can't save, and instead go into debt, you will quickly find yourself in financial trouble.

Don't kid yourself about savings. If you have $10,000 in your savings account and $10,000 in debt, *you have no savings.* And it's actually even worse than that. Because interest rates on short-term credit (as in credit cards) often run 18 to 21 percent, if you are making less than that on your savings, you have what is called *reverse leverage* (not a good thing). Reverse leverage compounds you into a financial grave, and you may not even see it happening until it's too late.

Again, spending wisely does not mean that you need to be a miser. Instead, you should review all areas of your life and learn how to reduce your spending comfortably. In the next few pages, we'll look at several strategies for spending wisely.

We've got to spend wisely and well. We have to put a hard question to ourselves before others put it to us: Do we need this item?

—Colin Powell

Don't worry if you can't use all of these strategies right now; we don't expect you to. We do, however, want you to read each one carefully so that you understand the concept that we are trying to teach. For example, just because you may not be ready to buy a car right now, don't skip over the ideas for saving money when you *do* buy a car. Why? Because, as noted in Chapter 2, developing good habits is one of the keys to achieving financial freedom. You should get into the habit of spotting savings opportunities so that you won't be limited to just these examples. You need to learn to *think like a saver.*

Wealth-Building Savings Strategy No. 1: Negotiate Tax-Free Raises

A 3 percent cost-of-living raise is nice. So is an annual bonus. But, instead of a raise or a cash bonus, ask your employer to pay for items that you can't deduct, but he can. This way, you won't have to pay additional income tax on the money you would have to earn to buy the item yourself, and your employer gets the deduction. This is the beauty of a tax-free raise. Examples of such expenses are dental cost reimbursement, personal medical deductibles, dependent insurance care, child care, and certain education costs.

Wealth-Building Savings Strategy No. 2: Live Your Retirement Years in a State That Has No Personal Income Tax

Look for retirement havens in states that don't have personal income taxes. Florida, for example, doesn't tax personal income. The people who move to Florida from a state that had personal income tax save a substantial amount in taxes every year—as much as 10 percent of their income. Obviously, this tax policy gives affluent individuals and families a big incentive to live in these income tax–free states. (And you thought people moved to Florida for the weather!)

Wealth-Building Savings Strategy No. 3: Execute Your Trades through an Online Discount Broker

With all the changes that are going on in the financial industry, there are now several types of stockbrokers. Full-service brokerage firms are the most expensive, discount brokers are the next most costly, deep-discount brokers are third, and "online brokerages" are the cheapest.

Never pay more for making the transaction than you need to. If you need individual advice, pay for it. If you don't need the advice, then use the cheapest provider that you can find. That will almost always be a deep discounter or an online provider. Depending on the number of trades you make every year, that could add up to hundreds of dollars saved. And a few hundred dollars saved each year adds up to thousands over the long term.

Wealth-Building Savings Strategy No. 4: Fund an IRA or Other Retirement Account Every Year

We've already discussed the necessity of establishing a long-term savings program. In order to take advantage of additional savings through tax deductions, make sure that at least part of the money you save is used to fund a retirement program such as an IRA. Based on the qualifications and specifications of the program, you will be able to generate additional tax deductions that will offset other income.

IRAs have been around for a long time now. For whatever reason, large numbers of people still neglect to fund them. Check out all of your options, including Roth and educational IRAs. (For more discussion, see Chapters 12 and 13, "Maximizing Your Retirement Plan" and "Invest in Your Child's Education.")

Wealth-Building Savings Strategy No. 5: Shift Income to Your Children to Reduce Taxes Paid

Instead of paying for all of your children's expenses, consider shifting assets to their name and letting them use the income from those assets to pay for their expenses. If your children have a tendency to spend all the money they can, you can protect this money by setting up a trust that you control for their benefit. The income produced will then be taxed at your child's lower tax bracket, which will result in a substantial savings to you over paying the money directly.

Another way to help your children is to pay them for any work they may do in your small business (there is more on this in Chapter 17, "Build Your Own Business"). They can use the money to pay their expenses, or, if they don't need it right away, they can begin funding their own IRAs at an early age. There is no minimum age for starting an IRA, so long as the child has earned income. Starting the IRA at an early age provides years of additional compounding and almost ensures a substantial nest egg when they retire. It is also a great way to introduce your kids to financial planning at an early age.

Wealth-Building Savings Strategy No. 6: Barter Your Services

Depending on your skill or trade, consider offering your services in exchange for something that you want or need. Professionals do this a lot, but the idea can be extended to almost any kind of business or service. This works best when you perform a certain task or job that is in high demand. For example, if you are a CPA or tax advisor, and a general contractor "hires" you at the same time you are using him to add a room to your home, then you can offer to exchange your services for his.

Over the years, we have exchanged services for trips, vacations, and even precious gemstones. However, if you receive bartered items in exchange for work, don't forget that the IRS considers this a taxable event, and you have to pay income tax on the value of the exchange.

Wealth-Building Savings Strategy No. 7: Join AAA and AARP to Get Discounts

No, we don't get a commission for persuading you to sign up with either of these associations. So our consciences are clear when we tell you that they provide *substantial discounts* on a lot of services. For example, in addition to a great roadside assistance service, AAA offers some of the best discounts on major hotels around the country. These discounts are frequently below the rates normally given as corporate rates, and it doesn't take long for them to add up to the cost of your annual membership fee. We take our AAA card with us every time we travel, and on almost all occasions, we get at least a 10 percent discount on the price quoted for a room.

To join the American Association of Retired Persons (AARP), you have to be at least 50 years of age. If you are, the cost of membership is only $12.50 per year and includes your spouse. There are many membership benefits and discounts, although you have to admit to being at least 50 to enjoy them. For more information, check out the AARP's Web site at www.aarp.org.

Both the AAA and the AARP have been around for a long time, and both have solid reputations with their members. The time will come when they will offer you insurance and other services. Here, as throughout this book, we recommend that you shop around. Maybe they have the best deal, and maybe they don't. Be a smart buyer!

Wealth-Building Savings Strategy No. 8: Check Your Property Taxes and File for a Reduction

Year after year, property owners are sent tax bills by the local assessor's office and are advised that their taxes will be increased the following year. Most homeowners do nothing because they see that the price given as the assessed value is lower than the current market price for their home. Frequently, out of fear of having their home reappraised at a higher price, they simply pay the new assessment.

Even if your town, city, or county assesses property at market value, it is common for the taxing entity to discount the value by a set percentage for all properties. Find out what that percentage is, and then decide if you agree with the value that has been placed on your home. Assessments must be applied evenly to all homes. If you think your assessment is higher than the assessments of other similar homes in your area, you should call your assessor's office and discuss the possibility of getting your assessment adjusted. To have the best chance, go down to your assessor's office and speak directly to the clerks. They really run most departments. They can give you a good idea of your chances for adjustment (often called "abatement") and also tell you how to file your request.

Also, don't forget to check whether you qualify for any tax discount. Many states have a homeowner's discount if your property qualifies as your official homestead. See what discounts you can qualify for.

A pint of sweat will save a gallon of blood.
—George S. Patton

69

Wealth-Building Savings Strategy No. 9:
Read Savings Books and Articles for New Ideas

Go to your local library or bookstore and get a copy of some of the classic books on savings that will show you how to get the best deals on everything. Examples include *Penny Pinching*, by Lee and Barbara Simmons (Bantam); *The Cheapskate Monthly*, by Mary Hunt (St. Martin's Press); *Living on Less and Liking It More*, by Maxine Hancock (Moody Press); and *Money Secrets the Pros Don't Want You to Know*, by Stephanie Gallagher (American Management Association). Each of these books has numerous additional small ideas about how to save money.

If you want to dig still deeper, go to Amazon.com and look at the other titles that come up when you look at those just listed. (And then look at the titles that pop up on those other pages.) Or, find one of these books at your public library and look at the other books next to it on the shelf.

Wealth-Building Savings Strategy No. 10:
Start a Home-Based Business

How does starting a home-based business help you save money? By giving you a multitude of ways to create additional tax deductions for yourself and your family. By changing your lifestyle to bring a business into your home, you can start to deduct things ranging from the business use of your car to entertaining friends who are also clients of your business.

There are so many real tax-reduction possibilities that even the smallest home business can pay for itself. (For more information on this, see Chapter 15, "Make Your Life Less Taxing," and Chapter 17, "Build Your Own Business," in Part 3 of this book.)

Wealth-Building Savings Strategy No. 11: Have a Will and Review Other Estate Plan Savings

Save your family money, headaches, and heartaches by preparing both a will and a living trust. You may not save any money while you are alive, but you will certainly save your children and other beneficiaries of your estate a lot of money and time *after* you pass on. Spend some time and money wisely now, while you are alive, and save on your estate taxes later by getting an estate plan done by a competent attorney.

If you have children who are minors, a will is essential, because it gives you the power to appoint a guardian for them should you die. Without the guardian appointment, the court will decide the fate of your children. (For more on this topic, see Chapter 16, "Build Your Family Financial Legacy.")

> *In this world nothing is certain but death and taxes.*
>
> —Benjamin Franklin

Wealth-Building Savings Strategy No. 12: Become a Part-Time Travel Agent

If you like to travel to faraway places, it may make sense for you to become your own travel agent. Of course, this is a personal decision, and it requires some genuine commitment on your part. It has worked out very well for us. We have put together tours to exotic places, and not only have we been able to travel free, but we've made money on every adventure. This is an excellent small business that you can start, and if you do, you can even deduct some of your other travel as well. One reason is that you have to keep scouting out new places to take your groups.

One important note of caution here: Throughout the book, we include dozens of ideas and strategies for building wealth and lowering your taxes. We would be remiss if we did not advise you to check with your accountant or financial advisor (if you have one) to make sure that all your deductions are completely legitimate. You will hear this mantra throughout the book: The key is to reduce your tax burden as much as possible, but to do so in a legal and ethical manner.

If you do decide to take the plunge into the travel business, you also become eligible for "fam trips," or familiarization trips, where you are the guest of the cruise line or resort, and it wines and dines you in an effort to persuade you to bring your groups to that particular destination.

You can find information about becoming a travel agent by going to www.astanet.com, sponsored by the American Society of Travel Agents. At this site, you can find out how to become a part-time home-based travel agent (or full-time, if you prefer).

Wealth-Building Savings Strategy No. 13: Cut Your Mortgage Term in Half

We will mention this again in Chapter 8, "Own Your Own Home," but if you already own a house, you can start saving money *now*. Contact your lender and ask whether your mortgage allows prepayments without penalty. If it does, ask your lender to run you an amortization table on your mortgage showing principal and interest payments by month.

Once you get your amortization table, make your regular payment each month *plus just the principal portion of your next month's payment*, as indicated on the table. Using this strategy, you'll save one-half the interest you would pay on a 30-year mortgage and have a free and clear property in 15 years.

Keep this strategy in mind the next time you refinance, as well. Always carefully compare the savings you get over the long term with the affordability of slightly higher monthly payments. After all, this is another forced savings plan that is fairly painless and very successful.

Wealth-Building Savings Strategy No. 14: Refinance Your Home

When interest rates drop at least two percentage points lower than your existing interest rate, it is time to refinance. Even if you have to pay additional "points" as the cost of refinancing, this is the rule of thumb for when you'll save money. You should also weigh carefully the actual cost difference for fixed- and variable-rate mortgages. You will have to compare the points charged for each loan and estimate the amount of time you will live in the property. Historically, fixed rates have been the better choice if you are planning to live in the property for at least five years after you refinance.

In recent years, interest rates have been at historic lows. This has allowed millions of homeowners to refinance and save significant amounts of money. Some have refinanced more than once. Some mortgage companies allow you to refinance with no additional closing costs at all. Before you take out a mortgage, ask your lender if that is the policy of her or his company. If it isn't, find a lending company that offers this important benefit.

Wealth-Building Savings Strategy No. 15: Join a Credit Union for Low-Interest Loans

Credit unions are cooperative financial institutions that are owned and controlled by the people who use their services. Credit unions are nonprofit, and therefore can offer many financing and insurance opportunities to their members at the lowest prices available. Look in your local Yellow Pages for the names of credit unions in your area, and contact them to see what you need to do to qualify for membership. You can also go to www.creditunion.coop for a listing of credit unions in your area.

Credit unions are excellent sources for car loans, and in recent years they have broadened their offers in other areas, such as insurance and residential mortgages. They are also a great way to do some quick and painless comparison shopping.

Wealth-Building Savings Strategy No. 16: Pay the Least in Taxes That the Law Demands

It is your right to do everything you can to reduce the amount of taxes you pay, as long as you are following the law. In order to save taxes, hire the best tax preparer you can. If you use a computer, learn how to use one of the tax programs available. (TurboTax is one, but there are many others. The purchase price is tax-deductible.) The companies that sell these software programs spend large amounts of money every year sniffing out the latest tax savings ideas, and these ideas are presented to you as you work through the program.

Behold the turtle. He makes progress only when he sticks his neck out.

—James Bryant Conant

Taxes are one of our largest expenses in life, as a percentage of income. It makes no sense not to explore every opportunity you have available to reduce your tax bracket. There will be much more in-depth information in Chapter 15, "Make Your Life Less Taxing."

Wealth-Building Savings Strategy No. 17: Increase Your Withholding Allowances to Reduce Your Tax Refund

Why give the IRS a tax-free loan? If you've been getting refunds every year, that's exactly what you're doing. You are losing the entire value of what that refund could have made for you during the year had you not overpaid your taxes.

If you're getting a refund each year, ask your employer to adjust your withholding by increasing the number of allowances on your W-4 form. Doing this will give you more money each month net in your paycheck. Don't spend that extra money! Add it to your savings plan on a monthly basis, and make the magic of compound interest work for you.

Wealth-Building Savings Strategy No. 18: Deduct All Your Health-Care Costs

It is clear that health-care costs are going to continue to rise at a faster rate than we can afford. Unfortunately, under the current tax code, you can't deduct your expenses unless they amount to more than 7.5 percent of your adjusted gross income. If you're striving for financial freedom, 7.5 percent of your adjusted gross income gets to be a big number.

If you are following our suggestions in this book, though, sooner or later there is a very good chance that you'll be starting a business for yourself. You'll want to incorporate the business for liability protection, but you'll also want to incorporate so that you can set up a corporate medical reimbursement plan. That's right: Even a small corporation with just one shareholder can set up a corporate medical reimbursement plan just like the big boys do. A corporate plan allows you to reimburse your employees for 100 percent of the cost of their medical expenses, with no deductible. This is true even if you are the only employee covered under the plan. Anyone in your family who also works in the business can join in the medical reimbursement plan and write off this expense.

In order to take advantage of this reimbursement for medical expenses, have your attorney draft the medical plan for you at the time of incorporation. It is only a short form, so you shouldn't have to pay more than $100 for it. You can also do it yourself by buying one of the self-help incorporation books on the market.

Wealth-Building Savings Strategy No. 19: Hold a Sale to Put Unproductive Assets Back to Work

The common garage sale has expanded to bigger garages, and now even affluent families are having fun and earning money by selling things that they no longer use. Consider making your sale an annual event, and encourage your friends and neighbors to join in by hosting their sales on the same day or weekend.

If you don't like the idea of a garage sale, then learn how to sell on eBay and hold your own auctions. In effect, you can use the Web as a giant front yard, in which you display your wares. The growth of eBay has been nothing short of astounding. According to eBay University, every day an additional 100,000 people around the world do business on eBay (on the buy and the sell side). As of 2005, it is estimated that there are 28 million sellers on eBay.

Consider saving the money you make from your annual sales or eBay auctions. While it may be tempting to spend the money you make from these sales, saving it will provide a better long-term return (of course, you have to pay taxes on the money you make on eBay just as you would on the profits of any other small business). For more information on using online auctions, go to www.eBay.com. For information on actually setting up your own business on eBay, we recommend the following books: *Building an eBay Business Quicksteps, How to Do Everything on eBay*, and *eBay for Dummies*.

Wealth-Building Savings Strategy No. 20: Use the Tax Exclusion on Homes to Generate Thousands of Dollars in Savings

If Chapter 8, "Own Your Own Home," doesn't motivate you to buy a home, the tax benefit will. Effective in 1997, all home sales qualify for a $500,000 exclusion from capital gains tax for married couples, and a $250,000 exclusion for singles.

This simply underscores the fact that your home is the best tax shelter in the world, and it gives you a huge extra incentive to own one over the years. It allows you to earn that money without ever having to pay any tax on the gain. We hope you love your home. But even if you don't—even if, for some reason, you can't stand it—view it as a forced savings plan that you don't have to pay taxes on when you sell (up to the limit).

In other words, a home is an *absolute necessity* for any would-be wealth builder. For complete information on the exact rules to follow when it comes time to sell, order the free IRS Publication 523, "Selling Your Home," which includes a good worksheet that can help navigate you through this. Call 1-800-TAX-FORM.

Wealth-Building Savings Strategy No. 21: Increase Your Loan-to-Value Ratio

When interest rates fall below 8 percent fixed, always try to negotiate as low a down payment as possible and conserve your cash for other investments where you can earn a higher return. With interest rates below 8 percent, you should be able to make more money using good investment strategies, and you will have leverage working in your favor. Let the bank earn (up to) 8 percent on the money it lends you, and put your money to work making *higher* returns.

This is an excellent strategy for your home or other real estate, because the loans and the savings are larger. But we apply it to *all* types of loans, including car loans and consumer loans, as a general rule of thumb.

Wealth-Building Savings Strategy No. 22: Use a Prepaid Legal Plan

You can save big money on legal bills by joining a prepaid legal plan. There are companies that sell prepaid legal advice in the same way that health carriers offer health insurance. You pay a small monthly premium, and in return, you get a reduction on any legal costs you have. Check the Yellow Pages of your phone book for the names of services in your area.

A big advantage of this service is just having an attorney available any time you have a quick question or need to have a demand letter sent out on your behalf at low cost. Just knowing you have an attorney available can sometimes stop people from trying to push you around.

One of the largest prepaid legal service companies in the country is Pre-Paid Legal Services, which is a public company. It operates nationwide and sells its program through individual direct sales.

Another source of information on these types of services is your local bar association. Typical costs for these services are approximately $26 per month for individuals (for businesses or corporations, the fees are understandably much higher).

Wealth-Building Savings Strategy No. 23: Reconsider Paying Out-of-State Tuition

Out-of-state tuition to private schools can be a disaster, in financial terms. Time and again, parents hock the family finances just to get their child into a favorite school. Consider this very carefully, if you and your family are facing this decision. Don't get sold on what you don't really need.

Look down the road a few years, and ask yourself, in as dispassionate a way as possible, if this *particular* school's degree will make that much difference. If it will, and if you're looking at a public university, investigate how your child can qualify for in-state tuition status after his or her first year in residence there.

Remember, either you or your child is going to be spending a large sum of money to make private schools or out-of-state schools possible. This is often a very emotional decision, meaning that it can involve more than just money. Run some numbers. If you were to take the difference between the tuition at an excellent state school and that at an excellent private school, and invest that sum at 12 percent, what kind of a financial start would those extra dollars give your child?

If you or your child has to go into debt for school tuition, the added interest will make your hardship even greater. Be cautious and prudent when selecting schools. Don't get caught up in emotion—or your costs may run away with you.

> *Once a decision was made, I did not worry about it afterward.*
>
> —Harry S. Truman

Wealth-Building Savings Strategy No. 24: Save Money When You Travel

Vacations are (usually) fun, but they can be very expensive. Here are four ways to save money on your next one:

1. *Work regularly with the same travel agent.* Let your travel agent get to know the types of trips you'd like to take, and ask him or her to be on the lookout for special bargains. One example is cruise lines that call travel agents at the last minute looking for customers to fill their ships. These last-minute trips are often deeply discounted from regular prices. Some cruise lines also offer last-minute discounts to former travelers, so don't forget to ask if your favorite does this.

2. *Be ready to be bumped.* Airlines are overbooking more and more. To solve the problem when it arises, they offer passengers free tickets and still get them out on the next flight. If you have the time, ask about the status of the flight when you first check in. If it is overbooked, give your name as an early volunteer. The airlines like this, because they don't have to make an overbooking announcement. You like this, because you'll be first in line for a free ticket.

3. *Call hotels direct.* Major hotel chains have 800 telephone numbers that you can use for convenience, but they are likely to cost you a lot more. This is because the local hotels often run discounts and other specials that the chain reservation service may be unaware of.

   By calling the individual hotel direct, you can often get a much better price. Speak to the desk clerk personally, because the clerk has the authority to discount room rates. While you are at it, don't forget to ask for the AAA or AARP discounts we discussed earlier.

4. *Shop aggressively online.* Check out the online travel services like Expedia.com or Cheapseats.com. These online companies cut special deals with hotels and airlines to get fares that may be available only online. You have to shop, but it is often very worthwhile.

Wealth-Building Savings Strategy No. 25: Buy No-Load or No Commission Security Investments

Many financial products, such as mutual funds or annuities, can now be bought "no-load," which means you pay no commission. Learning to buy this way allows you to invest more of your money directly into the product, because you eliminate some of the expenses that would otherwise eat away at your capital. If the product earns you money, you're adding even more money to your bottom line from the compounded returns because of the commission savings. Look for no-load mutual funds, stocks, and annuities, and even no-load life insurance.

Wealth-Building Savings Strategy No. 26: Adopt Valuable Safeguards

As more and more of the general public takes an active interest in investing, the number of frauds and scams will probably increase proportionally. Take special care to investigate before you invest, and consider these suggestions:

1. *Don't buy from a cold-call telephone solicitation.* It's too bad we have to eliminate phone sales from our options, but the chance of fraud is just too great. We're not suggesting that you stop doing business by phone—just don't make your initial business transaction based on one telephone call from someone you don't know.

2. *Don't buy under pressure.* If someone tells you that you *must* make a financial decision right then, walk away. There are very few opportunities that truly require an immediate decision, and the risk of a scam is too high. If you aren't given the time to make an intelligent decision, you will probably make a dumb one.

> *A man who will steal for me will steal from me.*
> —Theodore Roosevelt

3. *If the return being offered is a lot higher than the return anyone else is offering, there must be a (bad) reason.* The market sets acceptable returns for various risks. Since there are very few secrets in the investment world, if an investment is paying a high rate, then there is a correspondingly higher risk. Even if the deal is legitimate, it will definitely contain more risk, and chances are that if the rate of return quoted is very high compared to the return on other similar investments, the deal is not real. This falls under the "if it seems too good to be true, it probably is" rule.

Wealth-Building Savings Strategy No. 27: Avoid Waste and Create Lasting Savings

We all create waste in our lives. We throw out clothes that don't fit. We store things in our garage (or worse, pay to have them stored) for years, and many assets simply rot away. You get the idea. Instead of wasting anything, find someone or some organization that can put the asset to use. This includes your time as well as your possessions. You may not see a tangible benefit today, but we can assure you that you're building up a savings account in more important places.

YOUR MISSION TO WEALTH TO-DO LIST

1. REVIEW ALL OF YOUR CURRENT INSURANCE POLICIES, including life, health, auto, and business insurance, with your current agent, and ask specifically if he or she has suggestions that could help you.

2. TAKE A CLOSE LOOK AT YOUR CURRENT CREDIT CARDS. If any of them charge 18 percent or higher, transfer the balances of those credit cards to lower-rate cards.

3. IF MORTGAGE RATES FALL TO LEVELS AT LEAST 2 PERCENT BELOW YOUR CURRENT RATE, SHOP FOR A NEW LOAN TO REFINANCE YOUR PAYMENTS.

4. MAKE AN INVENTORY OF YOUR CURRENT ASSETS, AND RAISE MONEY BY SELLING WHAT YOU ARE NOT USING. Start a savings plan with the proceeds. If there are items that you cannot sell, donate them to thrift shops or your local church or synagogue. Make sure you get a receipt, and deduct the value of the item on next year's tax bill (make sure all receipts are kept in a place where you can find them).

5. BE CREATIVE. WITHOUT DRIVING YOURSELF CRAZY,
LOOK IN EVERY CORNER OF YOUR LIFE FOR WAYS TO
SAVE MONEY. Many of the tips in this chapter will save
you only small amounts of money. Collectively, though,
they can add up to a lot. (Remember: 100 percent of
the money you save drops to your bottom line, unlike
increased income!) Get in the habit of looking for
savings and bargains. But don't drive yourself crazy,
either. Part of the message of this book is that life is
supposed to be *fun* on the path to financial freedom.

★ ★ ★

CHAPTER 6

Wealth-Building Credit Strategies

*In preparing for battle I have always found
that plans are useless, but planning is
indispensable.*

—Dwight D. Eisenhower

One of the very good things about a credit card is that it represents perhaps the easiest and simplest way to access credit. No, not everyone can handle credit—or at least a lot, all at once. (Many people need to develop better habits first.) But the truth is that if you want to be financially free, you have to have good, solid credit, and you have to be willing to use it. In fact, being reluctant to access a line of credit (or never using a line of credit) actually works *against* your good credit rating.

In order to have a good credit rating, you have to have a demonstrated history of borrowing money and making timely repayments of your loan, regardless of what sort of loan it is: mortgage, car loan, home equity line of credit, credit card line of credit, and so on. Such a record of wide credit use is a valuable tool for building your financial freedom. It persuades other prospective lenders that you are a good risk—because you probably *aren't* a risk.

Let's assume that you are just starting out in the financial world. Let's assume that you don't have a bad credit record—in fact, you have no credit history at all. What should you do?

Credit Strategy No. 1: Build a Credit History

The easiest way to start building a credit history is through the use of a secured credit card. A secured credit card looks and works just like any other credit card, except that the issuer of the secured card requires that you place a deposit with it that is equal to the credit line extended to you on the card.

For example, if you want to have a secured credit card that has a $500 line of credit, you first have to deposit $500 with the bank that issues the card. You can then make charges of up to $500. Each month, you will have to pay your charges in full in order to keep the deposit amount where it was. By making timely repayments in full, you begin demonstrating your creditworthiness and begin to build an excellent credit record.

Secured credit cards are not something that you want to play games with. On the other hand, it's wise to understand the lay of the land out there. Because banking is a highly competitive business, many issuers of secured cards will actually grant you a line of credit that exceeds your deposit—usually between 110 and 150 percent of the value of your deposit. (Your $500 deposit, in other words, may be "worth" up to $750 in borrowing power.) In addition, issuers of secured cards will normally give you an opportunity to convert to unsecured status after a year or two of making timely payments on your account. There's no harm in asking in advance about the bank's policies regarding such a conversion.

Secured cards are also solid tools for those who need to *rebuild* credit ratings. Years of repayment problems often deprive people of the ability to get any sort of loan or credit line, even a small one, issued in the form of an unsecured credit card. The secured credit card is the best tool available to begin moving down the path toward positive consumer credit.

Buying on trust is the way to pay double.

—Anonymous

Credit Strategy No. 2: Use a Debit Card to Avoid Debt

Many careful, conscientious consumers like to use credit cards because of the ease and simplicity of carrying "spendable plastic." Credit cards eliminate the need to carry large amounts of cash around. They are more or less mandatory on the road, because rental-car agencies and hotels usually demand substantial security deposits to protect themselves against theft.

But plastic comes in several forms. In addition to the standard credit card, there is also a tool called a *check card* (or alternatively, a *debit card*). The check card looks just like a credit card (complete with either the Visa or the MasterCard logo), but it works like a plastic check. For every purchase you complete using the check card, in other words, the amount of the transaction comes right out of your checking account.

We should emphasize that check cards are *not* credit cards. In fact, they are the *opposite* of credit cards. But they are terrific financial tools, in that they (1) offer all the simplicity, convenience, and general usefulness of credit cards and (2) work like checks by not allowing you to spend beyond your means.

How to have your cake and eat it: Lend it out at interest.

—Anonymous

Maybe you already have both a credit card and a check card. If so, ask yourself if you're using those cards for different purposes. If so, why? If your (truthful) answer is that you use your credit card to buy things that you really can't afford, month after month, then you've hit on a cold, cruel financial truth about yourself: *You're living beyond your means.* Don't! Tell yourself that if you don't have the money to spend outright on something, then you can't have it. (The exception, of course, is major purchases such as cars or houses.) If you use your credit card, use it like a check card.

The only disadvantage to check cards is that your protections against check card fraud are less sweeping than your protections against credit card fraud. What does this mean? Stated simply, with a credit card, you are not responsible for more than $50 of fraudulent charges. But when it comes to a check card, it's possible for a bad guy to empty your checking account using a stolen card.

There is no standardized law currently in place that protects check card users in the event of fraud. If you already have a check card or are considering getting one for the first time, contact a customer service representative at the issuing bank to determine its policy on fraudulent use of the card. If you don't like what the representative tells you, you may want to shop around and get a check card from a bank with a more favorable fraud policy. This will require you to open a checking account at that second bank, but that's a small price to pay for increased security and peace of mind.

Credit Strategy No. 3: Reduce Your Credit Card Interest

One of the most important areas to explore for savings is credit and debt. At this point, we have to put our personal prejudices on the table: We absolutely *hate* credit cards. We use them, but we hate them. They can be the most expensive way to buy an item, and they lure more people down the path to financial ruin than any other single product or tool.

An excellent financial strategy to learn is to reduce your credit card debt. The cost of maintaining credit card balances, with interest rates ranging as high as 21 percent, is unreasonably high.

Even if your credit card company charges you a reduced rate of 16 percent interest, it will take you up to *seven years* to pay off a $1,500 credit charge if you pay only the minimum monthly balance. Seven years! Meanwhile, during those seven years, you will have paid almost the amount of the original charge again in interest. Your $1,500 purchase, in other words, will have cost you almost $3,000. How can anyone get ahead with that type of financial plan?

Carrying balances on your credit cards also triggers other "creative" clauses that work against you. For example, if you have a balance on your credit card, in most cases the "meter" on the interest charges begins running immediately from the day you make a new purchase, as opposed to the usual 30-day grace period. This increased interest compounding harms you in the same way positive compounding can help you: It just keeps adding up. Sooner or later, you find yourself sinking further and further into the debt hole.

Lack of orders is no excuse for inaction.
—George S. Patton

Credit Strategy No. 4: Avoid Hidden Credit Card Fees

If there is anything worse than high interest rates, it is the high fees that credit card companies charge you for making late payments. These fees can range from $20 to $30, even if you are only one day late.

If you calculate the late charge as a percentage of the amount of your payment, it certainly approaches what anyone would consider loan-sharking status. The lenders are able to get away with these charges because they classify them as penalties instead of interest. (Interest rates are more tightly regulated than so-called penalties.) Whatever you call it, late charges cost a lot of money, so make every attempt to pay on time. If you're juggling cash and you're unsure exactly how big a payment you can make, go ahead and make the minimum payment to avoid the late charge. You can always make an additional payment later.

Late fees aren't the only hidden costs that can get you. Credit cards also have terms and conditions in those little rulebooks that they send out (the little publications that no one ever, ever reads), and these terms and conditions can be very costly.

When you get to the end of your rope, tie a knot and hang on.

—Franklin Delano Roosevelt

Among the most atrocious are clauses that allow the issuers to increase your interest rate automatically if you are ever late on a payment. These jumps can go to as high as *24 percent* just for making one late payment. (As if 21 percent wasn't high enough!) If this happens, call and ask the issuer to roll back the interest rate immediately. Many times, it will. If it won't, try to pay off that card as fast as possible or transfer the balance to a lower-interest rate card.

Credit Strategy No. 5: Skip Credit Card Insurance

In Chapter 14 of this book, "Insuring Your Financial Future," we will review several kinds of insurance-saving techniques. One of the biggest savers, on a percentage basis, is getting rid of credit card insurance.

Simply put, this is insurance supplied by the credit card company to protect you if you lose your credit card. It doesn't usually cost very much (commonly under $25 for a year's coverage), but it's mainly a waste of money, because for the most part, you are already protected.

As noted earlier, credit laws say that you can't be charged more than $50 for unauthorized purchases made by someone else using your credit card. If you buy credit card insurance, you are protecting yourself against a loss of only $50 per credit card. Considered as a percentage of the risk, this is very expensive coverage, indeed. If you go two years without a loss by fraud—which, statistically speaking, you almost certainly will—you've broken even. If you go three years, you're ahead by $25. And every $25 counts!

Two other expensive add-ons are credit card disability insurance, which makes your credit card payments if you are injured, and term life insurance, which will pay off your credit card if you should die. These policies are also *very expensive* compared to other alternatives. Instead of the policies sold by the credit card companies, get regular disability or term insurance policies from an insurance company that you have investigated and found to have the best price.

Credit Strategy No. 6: Use Low-Interest Credit Cards Instead of No-Fee Cards

If you are able to pay off your card purchases each month, then you should use a card that charges no annual fee. The cards that offer the lowest interest rates (which is where you see the real savings if you maintain a running balance) will always be those that charge annual fees. The no-annual-fee cards will offer rates that are not as competitive. But if you pay off your balance each month, the interest rate won't matter.

Stated slightly differently, low-rate card issuers charge you an annual fee for the privilege of using their cards. But if you do not maintain a running balance, then interest rates become a nonissue. You're paying off your balance within the 30-day cycle, and you're never paying any interest on your purchases. So there's no benefit to you in having a lower-rate card with fees attached.

This discussion of fee-charging credit cards sometimes raises the question of why someone would bother using a credit card if she or he pays off the balance within 30 days. One answer, as stated earlier, is that there are some situations (rental cars, hotels and motels, Internet purchases) where credit cards are by far the easiest way to go.

The other reason (more important for our purposes) is that by using credit cards wisely, you demonstrate sound financial management. It helps you build a good credit history with the reporting agencies, as we have previously pointed out. And here's the part that really points toward financial freedom: By paying off the credit card balances within 30 days, an individual gets to use the card issuer's money for up to four weeks for free, while allowing his or her own money to continue earning interest in a bank account or investment account during that time. When you follow this strategy, you are using other people's money to make more for yourself.

OK, let's assume that we've persuaded you that you need a credit card. How do you pick one? The same way you make any other purchase: by shopping around. Just as you shop around for the best deals on cars, insurance, telephone serv-

It is one thing to see the forward path and another to be able to take it.

—Winston Churchill

ice, and a whole variety of other kinds of goods and services, you should shop around for the best deal on a credit card.

It is easy to find lists of the best current deals on cards. The lists are usually divided up between cards that assess an annual fee (lower-interest-rate cards) and those that do not (higher-rate cards). Using these lists, it is easier for you to determine which card is best for you, based on your specific buying habits and current circumstances.

There are two excellent places to look for these lists of credit cards. One is the Web site run by the Bank Rate Monitor (www. bankrate.com). This group tracks rates on everything from credit cards to mortgages, and everything in between.

For example, when we checked in July 2005, the credit spread on cards posted was from a low of 6.00 percent to a high of 20.40 percent! Two of the lows were Wells Fargo Bank (800-642-4720) and Wachovia Bank (800-922-4684). If you are not Internet-savvy, you can find these rates each month in *Money* magazine.

Once you have accessed your new card, stay alert. Don't get lazy. Keep shopping around. While a long credit history is better than a short one (we don't encourage you to engage in "card-hopping" practices), we *do* think that it's smart to look at the list of cards every year or two, just to review the rates. If you have a significant balance at that time, and you have the opportunity to drop at least two percentage points in your current rate, then moving to the lower-rate card may make a lot of sense for you.

Credit Strategy No. 7: Reduce Your Credit Card Balance

If you are an "average" American in terms of credit card use, then you probably have at least three credit cards, and your total balance across those three cards is at least $5,000. And if these figures represent the *average*, it means that there are a lot of families out there who are currently supporting many credit cards at one time, as well as associated balances totaling tens of thousands of dollars.

The situation dictates which approach best accomplishes the team's mission.

—Colin Powell

If you find yourself in a position where your credit card debt is beginning to become unmanageable, or if you've resolved to eliminate your ongoing credit card debt altogether, then it's time to adopt an effective strategy for paying off these bills once and for all.

There are two particularly effective ways to attack these debts. Each of these strategies is highly effective, as long as you commit to seeing your efforts through to completion.

Pay Down Credit Cards from Lowest Balance to Highest

The first strategy calls for you to pay down your credit card debts on the basis of lowest to highest balances. Let's say you have three cards, with balances of $500, $2,000, and $3,500. Using this strategy, you concentrate your efforts on paying off the $500 balance first. It's easiest to pay off the smallest balance first, right?

Once that balance has been eliminated, you move on to the next-highest balance, do the same thing there, and then repeat the process with the third (and final) balance. While you are making extra payments to bring down the one balance, make sure you at least make your minimum payments on the other cards to keep your good credit.

We like this strategy because it allows you to eliminate a card balance completely in the quickest fashion. Not only does this knock out an entire card, but completely eliminating one of your card debts will give you a big psychological boost. Remember, part of traveling the road to financial freedom is to feel good about yourself and enjoy your life. Cutting up a credit card can feel really good.

Pay Off the Cards with the Highest Interest Rates

The other strategy involves prioritizing your card debts on the basis of highest to lowest interest rate charged. You focus your efforts on paying off the card that charges the highest interest rate. Once you pay it off, you move to the card with the next highest rate.

This is also an effective strategy, because it focuses you on the card that, on a per-dollar-borrowed basis, is costing you the most. Your highest-rate card may also be the card with the highest balance, and it may take you longer to pay off this card than if you adopt the lowest-balance approach. The key here, though, is that you are eliminating your highest cost.

Credit Strategy No. 8: Convert Long-Term Debt to Short-Term Debt

As it has become more acceptable to use other people's money to purchase just about anything, banks, finance companies, and lenders of all types have "generously" sought to make your life easier by making those purchases "more affordable" through the use of extended terms (i.e., longer repayment periods). Extended loan repayment terms are popular because many borrowers focus on the size of the monthly payment rather than on the grand total that they are paying for whatever it is they are buying.

Would you live with ease, do what you ought, and not what you please.

—Benjamin Franklin

This can be a tremendous mistake. In general, a loan that runs longer than it has to costs you *far more* than it should and undercuts your efforts to achieve financial freedom.

Let's look closely at why extended loan terms can be so damaging to your bank account. If you buy a car for $20,000 and finance the purchase for 36 months at 9 percent interest, you will end up paying a total of $22,895 for your vehicle ($20,000 principal plus $2,895 in interest). If you finance that same purchase with a 60-month loan (still at 9 percent), you will pay a total of $24,910 for the vehicle. It's the same car, only now the bottom-line price tag is *more than $2,000 higher* because you opted to extend the term of your loan.

When you consider the number of cars you typically purchase over the course of a lifetime, it doesn't take long to realize that opting for the "standard" 60-month term is a money-losing proposition.

Now, it is true that with the 36-month option, your monthly payment is about $220 higher than if you finance for 60 months. That's the "savings" that so many consumers find appealing. But this savings is actually no savings at all, and it is in your best interests to stick with the higher payment in exchange for keeping thousands of dollars in your pocket over the life of your loan.

Term extensions occur all over the place, affecting all types of loans. Look at the home mortgage. Choosing a standard 30-year fixed-rate loan over the less common 15-year fixed-rate loan may be the single best example of sacrificing a significant sum of money by extending the term of the loan.

For instance, if you pay $100,000 for a home and finance the purchase with a 30-year fixed-rate loan at 8 percent interest, you will end up paying about $264,000 for the house when it's paid off. If you drop the loan term to 15 years at the same interest rate—which the bank will almost certainly do if it is asked to—you will pay a total of about $172,000 for the home. This is a savings of more than $90,000!

Here's the real kicker in the mortgage example. Your monthly mortgage payment on the 30-year loan is going to be about $733; with the 15-year loan, it will be about $955—higher, to be sure, but not so much higher that the 15-year loan becomes prohibitive for most people. In fact, it's an increase of only about 30 percent over the size of the 30-year payment (not 100 percent, as many people mistakenly believe).

The point should be obvious. By keeping loan terms as short as possible, you can easily realize a lifetime savings of well over $100,000. Amazing, right? It's even more amazing how few people take advantage of the shorter-loan-term option. Be smart. Borrow money for the *shortest term possible*. If you have long-term loans outstanding, look into converting them to shorter-term loans.

There are many ways to build your wealth over the course of your lifetime. But the best and first thing you can do to enhance your financial standing is to save money whenever possible. Keeping the term of your loan as short as possible will go a long way to helping you save large sums of money.

Credit Strategy No. 9: Avoid Debt Consolidation Loans

You've probably seen ads for "debt consolidation" loans. The reason you've probably seen them is that they are heavily advertised, which (if you stop and think about it) probably means that they are good moneymakers for the institutions that offer them.

Debt consolidation loans are typically offered by finance companies (as opposed to banks) and are specifically designed for people who are overburdened with consumer debt from multiple sources. A profile of a typical debt consolidation loan candidate is someone who has thousands of dollars in credit card debt from many different cards and may also have run up a big balance at department stores, consumer electronics stores, furniture stores, and the like.

The point of debt consolidation loans, as the name implies, is to combine all of your outstanding consumer debts into one lump sum so that you can make just one payment each month that goes to reduce the balance.

Besides the simplicity of the arrangement, the real selling point of debt consolidation loans is they also lower the total amount of money you have to pay toward your bills each month. In many cases, debt consolidation loans can cut your total payments in half or more. Well, who wouldn't want that—especially if you're feeling crushed by your debts?

Unfortunately, debt consolidation loans are not the panacea that they appear to be at first glance. True, they will make your life simpler, and they may slash your total monthly payments dramatically, but let's look at them more closely.

If you live among wolves you have to act like a wolf.

—Nikita Khrushchev

With a debt consolidation loan, the finance company pays off each of the debts you have with the various credit card issuers, furniture stores, and so forth, and you are left to pay the total balance back to the finance company directly. But this comes at a substantial cost.

First, the term of the loan is likely to be several years. Also, the interest rate on the loan is likely to be higher than the average interest rate you were paying on your debts individually. Even if the rate is roughly the same, the fact that you are now making these payments for several additional years means that the total amount of money you end up shelling out over the term of the loan will be *far greater*. Simply put, by spreading your total consumer debt over more years, the consolidation loan requires you to spend more in interest toward the repayment, even though your monthly payments are smaller (sometimes much smaller). It's the same principle as taking out a 30-year mortgage rather than a 15-year mortgage—and it's exactly the wrong direction to go in. It's converting short-term debt to long-term debt (see the discussion of term extension earlier in this chapter).

Another problem with debt consolidation loans is they can become the genesis of a "two-headed monster" that can easily devour careless, undisciplined consumers. What will you do if you suddenly have a wallet full of "live" credit cards again? Will you be disciplined enough to refrain from using them? Remember: The debt consolidation loan will pay off your *existing* debts, but it won't extend to any *new* debts you incur.

Consumers who use debt consolidation loans often find themselves in a far worse bind than they were in previously. As they begin to rack up new debt on the old cards, they now have to make *those* payments, in addition to the payments on the consolidation loan. If you do get a debt consolidation loan, *destroy the cards that got you into trouble in the first place*. That way, you can safeguard yourself against falling into this deadly financial trap.

YOUR MISSION TO WEALTH TO-DO LIST

1. BE A SAVVY CREDIT CARD USER. Learn the difference between credit cards and check or debit cards. Check www.bankrate.com for the best credit card for you.

Consider moving any high-interest debt to a card with a lower rate.

2. GET OUT OF CREDIT CARD DEBT. Adopt a specific strategy to pay down your credit card debt as soon as you can. Pay off the cards either from smallest to largest or from most expensive to least expensive. In either case, pay them off, and don't get into trouble with them again.

3. WHEN IT COMES TO BORROWING, THINK SHORT-TERM. Take a 15-year mortgage rather than a 30-year mortgage. (It's not as painful as it sounds.) Convert long-term debt to short-term debt. Avoid debt consolidation loans, which go in exactly the opposite direction.

★ ★ ★

CHAPTER 7

Advanced Credit Strategies

Good tactics can save even the worst strategy.
Bad tactics will destroy even the best strategy.

—George S. Patton

Credit—the ability to take possession of something today and pay for it later—is the currency of success. Without access to credit, few of us would be able to purchase a decent home or car. Indeed, it would be difficult for many of us to buy any high-priced consumer goods if we couldn't rely on credit. Used prudently and effectively, credit can be a powerful weapon in your financial arsenal.

Frequently, credit (especially in the form of credit cards) gets singled out as the cause of a person's financial woes. You hear, for example, that so-and-so "got into trouble because of all those credit cards." But that's like blaming the bent nail on the hammer rather than the carpenter. It's not credit that is the cause of money problems; it's the *misuse* of credit.

Still, it's not uncommon to hear people say proudly, "Oh, I *never* buy anything on credit" or "I don't owe on anything." Well, if these people have already achieved financial freedom, more power to them. If not, though, they're not being particularly smart. In fact, they're missing out on one of the best tools to increase their net worth, and meanwhile to enjoy more of what the consumer world has to offer. (Remember, one of our main premises is that you should *enjoy* your path to financial freedom.)

Just about every company in the world uses credit to pursue opportunities. If a company can borrow money at 5 percent and earn 10 percent on that money, while also increasing its market share, it doesn't make sense for the company *not* to borrow that money. Similarly, on the individual level, experienced investors often use credit to expand their portfolio holdings.

Some borrow externally—that is, from a bank or other source—and then put that money to work in their brokerage accounts. Others "buy on margin" (in other words, use the brokerage's money to buy additional shares of stock) to do the same thing. In short, there are a variety of ways in which credit can be used strategically to enhance the net worth of a business or individual.

Remember that credit is money.

—Benjamin Franklin

The upshot is that on many different levels and in many different ways, credit enhances your ability to move forward and build for the future. So if you have always looked at yourself as someone who is better off remaining completely out of debt, then it may be time to rethink that strategy. It may be time for you to embrace credit as a powerful financial tool, one that can both enhance your standard of living and help you build wealth.

Advanced Credit Strategy No. 1: Review Your Credit Report Free Once Every Year

Credit is not a right, but a privilege. Based on an individual's past borrowing history, he or she is deemed to be a good risk ("credit-worthy") or a bad one. Today, more than ever before, the creditworthiness of an individual is receiving serious scrutiny—either from a prospective employer or from a vendor who needs reassurance that a new customer will pay his or her bills on time.

Without a clean credit history, it is becoming more difficult for otherwise excellent employees to land better jobs, which in turn makes it more difficult for them to attain financial success. And consumers with poor credit are finding it increasingly difficult to secure basic services such as electricity and telephone service in their own names.

Given how important your credit history is to your financial success, it's extremely important that you *keep an eye on it*. Under a recent change in the Federal Fair Credit Reporting Act, you are now entitled to a free copy of your credit report once a year. Get it. The three national consumer credit reporting companies have now set up one central Web site and one toll-free help number. To order, click on www.annualcreditreport.com or call 877-322-8228. You can also write for a report at

ANNUAL CREDIT REPORT REQUEST SERVICE
PO Box 105281
Atlanta, GA 30348-5281

If you write, you will need to provide your name, address, social security number, and date of birth. If you have moved in the last two years, also include your previous address. We recommend that you call or go online in order to speed up the process.

You can get one report free each year from each of the big three reporting companies: Equifax, Experian, and Trans Union. There are two possible approaches: You can stagger the reports at different times—meaning that you'll get a different report every four months—or you can get all three at once.

The argument in favor of staggering the reports is that this gives you an early-warning signal about possible "identity theft." If you're the victim of identity theft, it means that someone has found a way to illegally charge purchases to your legitimate accounts or to open unauthorized accounts in your name. The sooner you know that this is going on, the better.

That being said, we still think it's best to request reports from all three reporting companies at once, and at the same time every year. This will let you compare the reports with one another. It will also establish a specific date each year when you review your credit history, making such a review as automatic as checking the batteries in your smoke detectors. We talked in Chapter 2 about good habits, and this is one of them. Here are the addresses:

TRANS UNION CORPORATION
800-916-8800
www.tuc.com

EXPERIAN NATIONAL CONSUMER ASSISTANCE CENTER
888-EXPERIAN (888-397-3742)
www.experian.com

EQUIFAX CREDIT INFORMATION SERVICES
800-685-1111
www.equifax.com

Although we may not admit it to ourselves, and although we may not consider it "fair," our credit history does say a lot about us. At least when it comes to money, our credit history can be a pretty good reflection (and predictor) of our habits and character. But—and this is an important "but"—it can be so only *when the report is accurate.*

The fact is, reporting agencies (also known as credit bureaus) have a reputation for making a lot of mistakes when it comes to consumer credit histories. It is all too common for someone who has never even paid a single bill late to learn that his or her credit report is full of negative entries—entries that obviously have no basis in reality.

> *The strength that matters most is not the strength of arms but the strength of character.*
>
> —Donald Rumsfeld

There are a lot of reasons that this can happen. All you really need to understand, though, is that it *can* happen. Because the quality of your credit report represents your "ladder of upward mobility," financially speaking, you have to make sure that the report is 100 percent accurate. So make it a point to review a copy of your credit report at least once a year, especially now that you can do it for free.

Finding and correcting mistakes is not the only good reason for reviewing your credit report. You should also do it to gain another perspective on your overall financial picture. Sometimes, that perspective can fill in blanks or prompt you to take needed actions. For example, in reviewing one of our own credit histories, we came across an open line of credit that we had simply forgotten about. We no longer needed access to that line of credit, so we closed it down.

Is this important? It can be. Continuing that example, if you have too many open lines of credit—*even if you haven't accessed them*—it can hurt your chances of getting the credit you *really* need in the future. Here's how it works: The lenders add up all the money you currently have access to, and if your total borrowing capacity appears to exceed your ability to carry that amount, even though you haven't borrowed a penny, they'll say no.

This is why you have to beware of things like stores that offer 10 percent off your purchase when you sign up for one of their store credit cards. Too many of these in your wallet may mean that you'll have a difficult time borrowing "more important" money in the future.

So, now that Congress has made it possible for you to get your credit report every year for free, *do it.* Don't leave anything to chance. We can't stress this enough. You would be amazed at how many people have had their lives thrown into turmoil because of negative entries that erroneously showed up on their credit reports—even people with very modest, mostly inactive credit histories. Catch mistakes. Close any unnecessary open lines of credit. Take responsibility for your own credit history.

Advanced Credit Strategy No. 2: Dispute Inaccurate Entries

If, after reviewing your credit report, you decide that it contains inaccuracies that reflect negatively on your credit history, it's time to take action. Specifically, you'll want to dispute the offending entries with the credit bureau.

There are three ways you can dispute inaccurate information on your credit report. One is to use the bureau's own dispute form, which will be included with the copy of the report you receive. Another is to write a letter that explains to the credit bureau that you are disputing a specific entry. Finally, you can file a dispute online or by calling the bureau's customer service.

Once you initiate the dispute of an item on your credit report, the bureau has 30 days to either verify the claim or remove the inaccuracy, according to the provisions of the Fair Credit Reporting Act. While the credit bureaus are usually very good at removing verified inaccuracies promptly, don't take anything for granted. Make sure to request a copy of your *revised* credit report showing the corrected mistake.

If 30 days have passed and you have not heard anything from the bureau you are working with, contact it again. These days, the agency representatives will probably be very apologetic and should help you to resolve your case quickly. If that does not happen, however, then you should send the agency a certified letter demanding resolution of your case, as well as proof of that resolution, within seven days.

Mention in your letter that if you do not hear from the agency within that time, your next course of action will be to contact the Federal Trade Commission (FTC) to file a formal complaint. If that doesn't work, follow through. Contact the FTC at (202) 326-3650 or at www.ftc.gov. It will respond.

It is important to be diligent about resolving any inaccuracies as quickly as possible. There is nothing worse than being hamstrung by

When you want to fool the world, tell the truth.

—Otto von Bismarck

negative entries that don't belong to you. Review your report, note any inaccuracies, and waste no time in working to eliminate them.

Advanced Credit Strategy No. 3: Deal with the Credit Agency Not the Creditor

One of the mistakes that people with credit problems commonly make is to contact the creditor who posted the entry in the first place. On the surface, that seems like a logical course of action, right? A quick call or a brief letter to the original creditor should resolve the matter, shouldn't it?

Unfortunately, that isn't usually the case. The first thing to remember is that inaccurate entries can end up on your credit report for a variety of reasons. While it is certainly possible that the creditor simply made an error when it notified the credit bureau, it's just as likely that the error was made by the bureau itself.

Credit bureaus are simply businesses that have come up with ways to keep track of the credit histories of millions of individuals and businesses. This means that in their offices and on their computers, there's a *lot of information* flying around. It also means that they make mistakes—for example, by assigning a negative entry to the wrong person. In those cases, the creditor will be of absolutely no use to you. Only the credit bureau can correct the problem.

Another reason you should take up your grievance with the credit bureau has to do with the law. The dispute provisions of the Fair Credit Reporting Act (FCRA) apply to the credit reporting agencies rather than to the creditors themselves. So any leverage that you gain by citing the FCRA works only with the agencies. Go directly to them.

Advanced Credit Strategy No. 4: Have "Old" Entries Removed from Your Credit File

One of the most pressing issues for individuals who have negative information on their credit reports is the *length of time* that negative information remains in the report. According to the provisions of the FCRA, negative information that is more than seven years old is not supposed to appear on your credit report. If you find that there is such an entry, then contact the credit bureau immediately about having it removed. You will be given a case number, and your dispute will be handled in much the same way that a dispute over inaccurate entries is treated.

We should note the one exception to the seven-year rule. Bankruptcies may remain on your credit report for up to ten years. So if you have a bankruptcy reflected on your credit report that is older than seven years but not older than ten, then its appearance on your report is not a violation of the FCRA. If more than ten years have passed since the bankruptcy, then by all means be as proactive as you can about having the entry removed.

Advanced Credit Strategy No. 5: Be Aggressive with the Credit Bureau

The people who staff credit bureaus are no different from most of the other service people we encounter in an average day. Many of them feel overworked, underpaid, and underappreciated. They often see their jobs chiefly in terms of the paychecks they provide. So it's *your* job to keep a very close watch over the investigations taking place with respect to your credit report.

Do not allow the credit bureau to be lax and take longer than 30 days to respond to your dispute. Stay on top of it. Feel free to contact the bureau via telephone or e-mail to get an update on your situation. We suggest going to the trouble and limited expense of making your follow-up inquiry via certified letter. If you send certified letters, you have a record of your correspondence with the credit bureaus, which is important should

> *Plans don't accomplish work. Goal charts on walls don't accomplish work. . . . It is people who get things done.*
>
> —Colin Powell

it become necessary to prove both that you contacted the bureau and when you did so.

Advanced Credit Strategy No. 6: Demand the Removal of Unauthorized Inquiries

At the end of your credit report is a section called *Inquiries*. This section details who has reviewed a copy of your credit report and when they did so. If an entity is interested in reviewing your credit report, it is supposed to get your permission before doing so, but there are a lot of loopholes to this. If you access a copy of your credit report today, you will probably find the names of businesses completely unrecognizable to you that have accessed your credit report.

Rather than waste a lot of time becoming indignant about the inappropriateness of these businesses taking it upon themselves to access your credit report, just dispute the inquiries as you would dispute anything else. These inquiries will be especially easy to dispute and have removed if you have never given your permission to have your report reviewed in the first place.

The reason it is important to have the number of inquiries indicated on your report kept to a minimum is that creditors tend to dislike giving credit to people whose credit reports reflect a lot of inquiries. Having a lot of inquiries suggests that you may be a person who takes the responsibility of credit very lightly and tries to get more as often as you can.

To the credit bureaus, this indicates that you are someone who might be unable to repay your debts in the future. This could well lead to a lower FICO score (see page 113) and hurt your chances for credit. It isn't fair, of course, that these inquiries end up on your report the way they do, but don't sweat it; just have them deleted.

Advanced Credit Strategy No. 7: Update Your Credit File with Positive Information

There are basically two types of positive information that we encourage you to add to your credit file, as appropriate. The first type of positive information is any sort of credit account (credit card accounts, mortgages, any kind of loans) on which you've been making timely payments or that is otherwise a positive reflection on your credit payment history. Just as credit bureaus can make errors by including negative information that isn't supposed to be there, they can make errors by omitting positive information that belongs on your report.

Your strategy here is to contact the credit bureau right away to inform it of any positive credit relationships that are missing from your file. Be prepared to provide all the relevant information about missing account(s), such as the names of the creditors, the account numbers, amounts, and dates. Just as the credit bureau will have to verify the entries you dispute, it will have to verify this information as well. Once it does, the information will be added to your report.

Advanced Credit Strategy No. 8: Add Your Own Comments to Your File

Another way to improve your credit report is to provide information regarding mitigating circumstances that may surround any of the negative information in your file. The only thing your credit report reflects is the cold, hard facts, such as that your payments on one of your accounts fell 60 days behind. It is your right to augment such an entry with whatever information you can about the circumstances surrounding the late payments that may soften the blow of the information itself.

For example, were you unemployed during the period you fell behind? Were you living out of the country during that period, and the creditor's bills never reached you? Make certain that any relevant information like that makes it into your credit file. Its appearance in your file will not change your credit score, but it could make a difference to prospective employers or other people who use credit reports, such as apartment leasing companies.

Advanced Credit Strategy No. 9: Review a Copy of Your Credit Report for Free If You've Been Denied Credit

If you made a formal application for credit and were turned down, a written notification of your denial will inquire whether you want to review a copy of your credit report. The opportunity to receive a free copy of your credit report whenever you are turned down for credit is law, and it is a great way to review your credit history more than once a year without having to pay for a copy of the report.

What's more, if you applied for credit in the first place, you probably did so in the belief that your request would be approved. Consequently, if you were denied, you would do well to see just what your report looks like, especially before you make another application for credit elsewhere. You should never pass up the opportunity to review your credit report for free.

Some people believe that the first casualty of any war is the truth. But in this war, the first victory must be to tell the truth.

—Donald Rumsfeld

You'll want to get a copy of the report from the credit bureau that the lender used to make its decision. The lender is required to share that information when you are turned down. Write the agency and include a copy of the rejection notice. Your letter should simply explain you were turned down for a loan based in part on its credit report and that you would like a free copy of that report.

Advanced Credit Strategy No. 10: Be Cautious of "Credit Repair Services"

Because of the importance of having good credit, new businesses have cropped up that charge fees for cleaning up your report. Some of these businesses are legitimate, and some are not. Remember, after reading the information in this chapter, you know what you can do for yourself, so it may be unnecessary to pay money to someone else.

Advanced Credit Strategy No. 11: Improve Your FICO Score to Build Your Credit

Last but not least, let's talk about something called a *FICO score*. Chances are you have one, and chances are you've never heard of it.

Your FICO score both reflects and influences your financial well-being. This score, which is determined by a company called the Fair Isaac Corporation, also affects whether you qualify for an apartment, and it can even make the difference in getting a job. It is the single most important financial metric that people will judge you on. A higher FICO score means lower interest rates on everything from credit cards to mortgages.

Your FICO score is based on your spending habits, where you live, how much you make, and how much you owe. The score ranges from 720 to 850 on the high end, and 500 to 559 on the low end. The higher your score the better.

Why does this matter? The answer lies in two words, as suggested earlier: *interest rates*. At current rates of interest, a person with a high FICO score can borrow money at rates up to 3.5 percent lower than someone with a low FICO score. On a $20,000 loan, that translates into a difference of $103 per month.

Obviously, you don't want to be one of the people paying that extra $103 per month. You need to (1) find out your score, (2) work to get it as high as possible, and (3) work to *keep* it there.

Your first step in FICO score improvement is to get a copy of your score by getting a copy of your credit report, as we previously discussed. You can also go to www.MyFICO.com and get your score directly from Fair Isaac for a small charge.

OK, now you know where you stand. Let's assume that you want a higher FICO score. Let's also assume that you've already taken the necessary steps to fix any flat-out mistakes in your credit history, as discussed earlier. Here are other things you can do to improve your overall credit picture:

1. *Build credit if you don't have any.* No, this doesn't mean that you should run out and buy everything you can on credit. It *does* mean that you should work on getting one or two of the major credit cards—like MasterCard, Visa, or American Express—and begin to use those cards wisely. *Make payments on time.* It is better to pay the minimum amount due on your account on time than to pay more and be late on the payment date.

2. *Keep your debt-to-credit ratio as low as possible.* This means that the total debt on your cards should be as low as you can keep it compared to the credit limit allowed. A high credit line with low usage is positive.

3. *Don't try to get a lot of credit at once.* In other words, don't run right out and try to get multiple credit cards.

A lot of activity at one time makes credit people nervous. Their computers may conclude that you have a financial problem and lower your score.

4. *Pay attention to history.* The longer you have credit with people, the more you look like a good risk. So once you get a card, keep it. We made a mistake on this front once. We cancelled some older credit card accounts, on the assumption that this would be a good, conservative move. It wasn't. Why? Because it simultaneously eliminated our good history and increased our debt-to-credit ratio. As they say, sometimes you can't win for losing.

YOUR MISSION TO WEALTH TO-DO LIST

1. GET A COPY OF YOUR CREDIT REPORT. Immediately order a copy of your credit report from one of the three major credit bureaus. This is your right, under the law. Better yet, get a copy from *each* of the credit bureaus and compare them. Do this at the same time every year.

2. IF THERE ARE MISTAKES ON THAT REPORT, GET THEM FIXED. Use the leverage of the FCRA to get the credit bureaus to straighten out your record. If they don't respond as they're supposed to, report the situation to the Federal Trade Commission.

3. FIND OUT YOUR FICO SCORE. This is absolutely critical. You need to understand your starting point.

4. RAISE YOUR FICO SCORE, AND KEEP IT RAISED. Higher FICO scores translate directly into lower interest rates. Establish a credit history, if you don't have one. Develop and stick to good credit-handling habits. Track your score as it rises—and celebrate your success!

★ ★ ★

CHAPTER 8

Own Your Own Home

I never want to pay for the same real estate twice.

—George S. Patton

Home ownership has long been a cornerstone for building wealth in America. Unfortunately, from the mid-1980s to the early 1990s, in many parts of the United States, many people decided not to buy homes because of the softness in the housing market.

This proved to be a mistake in the long run, because the housing market has been on fire during the last few years. As the stock market tanked in the early 2000s, real estate prices soared. Also, low mortgage interest rates brought monthly payments down to levels that amount to little more than the payments for rental apartments or condos.

New mortgage programs are also helping first-time buyers (and so-called nontraditional borrowers) come up with down payments in creative ways. For example, one popular new program includes the issuance of a simultaneous second mortgage by the same lender. The second mortgage covers all or part of the down payment.

If you have never owned a home, consider making the move now. Given the favorable interest-rate environment, your opportunity is the best it's been in years. In many major markets across the country, double-digit growth has made home buying a very smart move indeed. Even in the vast majority of "softer markets," home appreciation still beats inflation by one or two percentage points. Appreciation, combined with low down payments, means positive leverage that works in the homeowner's favor.

A quick example illustrates the point. The median price of an existing home in 2005 is about $193,000 (see www.Realtors.com). A 10 percent down payment is $19,300. Property values nationwide are expected to appreciate by 5 percent per year.

Remember, though, that appreciation applies to the *total value of the home*. In our example, the annual appreciation for one year would be $9,650. Compare that return to your cash investment of $19,300 (the down payment), rather than to the total value of the home, and you have an annual rate of return of 50 percent. Very few investments yield that large a return.

Of course, this simple illustration doesn't take into account your monthly payments, taxes, and insurance, but these are offset by the fact that you aren't paying rent somewhere else. In addition to the high rate of return, you also get to deduct the interest you pay from your federal taxable income, and you will pay no tax on your first $500,000 of capital gain (joint owners). And then there are the intangibles. You and your family have a home of your own—the American Dream. You have a safe base of operation for all of you.

In addition to all of these advantages, common sense tells you that you have to live *somewhere*. If you rent, you will pay and pay, and wind up with nothing. If you buy, you will ultimately have a nest egg of your own free and clear because your payments reduce your mortgage. For that reason alone, you should take the plunge and buy a home *as soon as you can.*

Some home-buying processes change over the years, but most do not. In this chapter, we share home-buying strategies that have stood the test of time and can be adapted to a great variety of situations.

Never yield ground. It is cheaper to hold what you have than to retake what you have lost.

—George S. Patton

Home-Buying Strategy No. 1: Keep in Mind That Location Is Everything

There is an old axiom in the real estate business that the three most important factors are location, location, and location. It's true. Always buy in the best neighborhood you can afford.

First, though, establish how much you can afford. Once you have established that number, you are far better off buying the smallest house in an expensive neighborhood than the biggest house in a lower-priced neighborhood.

The logic is straightforward: The higher prices in the expensive neighborhood will tend to pull the price of your home up as they appreciate. If homes in the lower-priced neighborhood lose value, the value of your home will drop with them, and it may become difficult to sell. We have heard some real estate horror stories over the years, and plummeting prices were almost always the result of a particular neighborhood declining in value.

Similarly, another great home-buying strategy is to buy the least expensive house on the street. As a rule, this allows you to realize more gain from any home improvement or remodeling, since you will be less likely to overbuild for your neighborhood.

Home-Buying Strategy No. 2: Investigate the Schools

Neighborhood amenities are also important considerations. One of the most important is the reputation of the school district. Avoid buying into a neighborhood in a weak school district, if you can. While you cannot do anything if the quality of the schools in your neighborhood slips over time, knowingly buying into a neighborhood with weak schools is a mistake.

Overcrowding in the schools has forced our children to attend some unusual schools, to say the least. When you're buying a home, don't assume that the school down the street is the one that your child will attend. Call the school board, give it the address of the property you propose to buy, and find out which school district that house is in. Access to specific schools can be very important to future buyers, so being in the right district can dramatically affect your future resale value.

MORE HOME-BUYING TIPS

Home-Buying Strategy No. 3: Consider Resale Value

Everyone has his or her own tastes and preferences when it comes to homes, so we won't presume to tell you what sort of house to buy. But to maximize the return on your investment, there are some guidelines to consider. We'll look at some of the most important ones in the pages that follow.

It is important that you buy the kind of home that will appeal to the largest possible number of buyers. An unusual home with a unique design may look good to *you*, but when it comes time to sell, that offbeat look may turn off potential buyers. So keep it in mind going in that unusual designs will limit your market and potentially hurt the resale value of your home.

You should also consider other factors that affect potential resale value. For example, there is a bigger market for four-bedroom homes than for three-bedroom, and for three-bedroom homes than for

The time to repair the roof is when the sun is shining.

—John Fitzgerald Kennedy

two-bedroom. Also, the more bathrooms, the better the resale value. Having two bathrooms is now considered almost a necessity, and an extra half bath (a powder room) helps both while you live in the house and upon resale.

Home-Buying Strategy No. 4: Order an Independent Home Inspection before You Buy

Before entering into a contract for a home, be sure to have it inspected. Sure, home inspection is another cost, but having an expert evaluate the home you are buying for structural and other problems is a cheap form of insurance. Even if you are qualified in this area yourself, it is best to bring in an outside expert, since we all get caught up in the excitement of buying a new home.

Mistakes can add up quickly and get very expensive. Let someone unbiased represent you in this part of the process. If that person finds problems, insist in the contract that the seller pay for the cost of the repair.

Also, if you can, get a good home warranty. Remember, once the deal closes, it's hard to get any money back.

Trust, but verify.
—Ronald Reagan

If you are using a realtor, ask that person to suggest a reputable home inspection company. If you are buying on your own, check for national companies that have a local presence in your area. And remember, a warranty is only as good as the reputation and stability of the company you are buying from.

Home-Buying Strategy No. 5: Use a Buyer's Broker

Buyer's brokers are a relatively new phenomenon. Historically, the vast majority of buyers have worked with real estate brokers who were working for the *seller*. This has created hard feelings and some unhappy results for buyers who thought the broker showing the house worked for them. The new trend is for brokers to clearly designate which side of the transaction they are representing. So if you're buying, work with a buyer's broker, who will be looking out for *your* best interests.

As a rule, we suggest that you find the most experienced real estate professional to represent you. Because the fees are generally the same throughout the industry (that is, they're generally not based on the broker's degree of expertise), it doesn't cost you any more to work with the best.

An experienced and successful broker will know more about the market and how much you should pay for a home. He or she can help you negotiate to get the best price. The broker will also have contacts with experienced lenders, title companies, insurance companies, and real estate lawyers. By using proven professionals, your buying experience will be smoother and more successful.

Where do you find the best brokers? Start with the local Board of Realtors. Ask for a list of brokers in the area who have an

Accredited Buyer Representative (ABR) designation. This designation is sponsored by the National Association of Realtors and can be used only by agents who have received special training and been certified in buyer representation. Then ask for the names of the top five buyer's brokers on that list, based on sales volume. Interview each of them and pick the one with whom you are most comfortable. This takes some time, yes—but it will definitely pay you back.

THE INS AND OUTS OF GETTING A MORTGAGE

Why is it that people who will drive across town to save money on a toothbrush won't shop for financing on a $100,000 home? It doesn't make sense. Given the wide disparity in mortgage costs today, you simply cannot afford *not* to shop for the best deal. By doing so, you will save yourself many thousands of dollars over the life of your mortgage.

Home-Buying Strategy No. 6: Shop for the Best Terms on Your Mortgage

There are several ways to shop for your financing, and we recommend that you follow a combination of all of them. Start by looking in the local newspaper. Most papers print a weekly summary of mortgage rates in your area, and this summary includes most of the information you'll need in order to start comparison shopping.

Then start calling national banks that have a presence in your market. Simply pull out the Yellow Pages and start shopping. Tell them the approximate size of the mortgage you are looking for, and they will tell you about some of the basic financing plans they have available. Even if you don't ultimately do business with them, it will give you a second opinion on the competitive rates and terms.

The third shopping method is to use a mortgage broker to represent you. Make sure you are working with a broker who represents multiple financing sources, not one who's simply a captive broker for a single lender. You want the broker to use his or her expertise and to shop for your loan by submitting it to several lenders.

The fourth strategy is to shop online. There are now some excellent sources for mortgage shopping, and the offers we have seen have been good. One source to start with is www.lendingtree.com. Online companies like Lending Tree will ask you to complete an extensive credit application, which they send out electronically to the lenders they work with. Based on the application and your credit report—which they will obtain—you will get specific offers from those lenders that qualify you for the loan.

If you find you are having trouble getting a loan, it may be because of something in your credit report. If you are turned down for a loan, you can get a free copy of the credit report that the lender used to make its determination. Make sure you order the report to see if there is a problem, and also to determine if the report is even accurate. As noted in the previous chapter, these reports are notorious for containing errors, so don't be surprised if you find some. If you do find mistakes in the report, write directly to the reporting agency to dispute the mistake.

A word of caution: If you are using recommended mortgage professionals, you're unlikely to run into an unscrupulous broker. (A recommendation from a friend or your accountant is a good starting point.) But stay alert. Avoid anyone who asks for big upfront money in order to help you get a loan.

Normally, mortgage brokers will charge a fee that is built into the loan. To compare this fee and all of the other charges you will pay for the loan, ask for the quoted annual percentage rate (APR). The APR on a mortgage gives you a true number to use in comparing one loan with another—it is the true

Associate with men of good quality if you esteem your own reputation.
—George Washington

rate after all of the interest, points, and fees have been added in.

Home-Buying Strategy No. 7: Compare Loan Types

While shopping for a mortgage, you will learn about fixed-rate and adjustable-rate mortgages with a variety of time spans attached to them. Don't assume that the typical 30-year fixed-rate mortgage is your best bet. There are plenty of other options to consider.

When you are buying a home in a low-interest-rate environment and rates are rising, get a fixed-rate mortgage, or at least one that gives you the option of fixing the rate at a later date. The interest on a fixed-rate loan stays the same over the life of the loan, while that on an adjustable-rate loan changes at different stated intervals of time.

For example, in mid-2005, it is possible to get a 30-year fixed mortgage at around 6 percent. However, on a five-year adjustable-rate mortgage, you may be able to snag the loan for just over 4 percent. If you are sure that you will keep the property for five years or less, take the adjustable-rate loan. But if you are not sure, it's probably better to get a fixed-rate loan and eliminate your exposure to future interest-rate hikes.

If you get a fixed-rate loan and rates do go down, you can always refinance at a later time. If you get an adjustable-rate mortgage and rates rise, not only will your monthly payments increase, but there is a chance that if rates rise substantially, you might not qualify for new fixed-rate financing, and you would be stuck in a mortgage with rates going up every year. That is a situation that you should take great pains to avoid.

Over the years, there have been many games played with adjustable-rate mortgages, including "teaser rates" (extremely low rates tied to an index that increases your interest rate in a year) and "balloons" (mortgages that simply end after a short period of time, requiring you to start over). Be careful about taking on one of these loans, particularly if you think you may live in the home for more than a few years.

If you can afford the higher monthly payments (about 30 percent higher), consider a 15-year mortgage instead of a 30-year mortgage. For the relatively small increase in payments, you will pay off your loan in half the time and pay half the interest. This can add up to an amazing amount of savings over the life of the loan.

If you are unsure about making the higher payments, get a 30-year mortgage that allows you to make additional payments to reduce the principal. Make sure that all prepayments apply to reduce your principal, and that extra payments don't just count as an interest payment or a regular payment. With this type of loan, you can make an extra "principal only" payment whenever you can, without the pressure you might feel from a 15-year mortgage—and you'll still be able to knock months or years off the mortgage, depending upon how much you are able to contribute each month.

If making extra payments on a 30-year fixed mortgage becomes a problem, you can simply skip the extra payments. But people who begin to skip the extra payments often find it difficult to get back into that good habit. That's just human nature, so we recommend that people make those extra payments as consistently as possible.

Another idea is to pocket the payment difference between the 15-year and the 30-year mortgage. For example, go ahead and get the 30-year mortgage, but take the difference in payments and use that amount to fund an investment program. By doing this, you gain diversification and don't have everything tied up in real estate. Set the investment payment on an automatic draft to keep you regular each month. This means working with your brokerage firm or bank to have a certain amount of money taken out of your checking account each month and used to purchase shares in a mutual fund or other investment vehicle.

Which of these three options is best? That depends on your personal circumstances and your level of self-discipline. The point is that you *do* have options, and you *don't* have to automatically select the 30-year loan.

Home-Buying Strategy No. 8: Compare the Benefits of Buying a New Home versus an Existing One

There will always be a running debate about which type of home is better: new construction or an existing home. The truth is that there is no definitive answer. It is likely that on a square-foot basis, a new home will cost you more, because building costs have gone up in recent years. On the other hand, modern amenities found in new homes—such as larger interior spaces and upgraded kitchens and bathrooms—are appealing and will also work to your advantage when it comes time for you to sell the property.

Our suggestion is that you look at both older and new homes. You'll have an up-close look at the advantages and disadvantages of each, and you'll quickly develop your own preferences. There is no one right answer for everyone, so take the time to look at a good number of homes and pick what *you* like best.

If you are handy with a hammer and toolbox, then you can buy an existing home and increase its value through what is called "sweat equity." This is an excellent way to build value, and it's the equivalent of having a second job or starting a small business. In

Structure depends on strategy; strategy is determined according to events.

—Sun Tzu

fact, we have known many people who have had such a great time doing this that they have bought one or two houses a year just to fix them up and sell them at a profit. But if you can't imagine anything worse than spending your evenings and weekends working on a fixer-upper, a new home is probably the best choice for you.

Home-Buying Strategy No. 9: Use Real Estate as a Way to Diversify

Real estate investing schemes are regularly promoted on TV as the solution to your financial woes. These ad campaigns have led many people to ask us whether real estate is a good investment or a scam.

The short answer is that real estate investing can be an excellent way to diversify your financial holdings. And yes, it *is* possible to buy real estate with "no money down." Buying and selling homes can also be a good second career. Understand, however, that all this requires a lot of work, can bring a lot of worry, and will *not* turn you into a millionaire overnight. However, it is one of the fastest ways to build wealth today.

We have both been very active with our real estate investing over many years. We have made money and lost money, but we have had a great time along the way. When you do it just right, real estate investing can produce big rewards, even if you have only a small amount of working capital.

Real estate is also an investment that produces additional opportunities because of the leverage provided by financing. You can start out with little cash and build a relatively large investment portfolio. But *timing* is extremely important. Real estate always has "boom" and "bust" cycles. It is therefore critically important that you do all of your homework, to make sure that you don't get caught holding the bag (or an expensive home) in the midst of a bust cycle.

If you're interested in investing in real estate, we encourage you to check out your local community college for relevant courses. In addition, almost all major cities have local real estate investor groups, where you can make contacts with people who are already buying and selling properties for a living.

> *We must always know exactly what we know and what we do not know. Never get the two confused!*
>
> —George S. Patton

ADVANCED MONEY-SAVING REAL ESTATE STRATEGIES

Once you gain some experience in the real estate market, you may want to consider one or more of the following additional strategies.

Home-Buying Strategy No. 10: Be Your Own Broker

If you're going to get involved in real estate, it may prove worth your while to get a real estate license. Many local real estate offices offer classes leading toward this goal.

Some states have stiff requirements for getting a license, and you may consider the time commitment too dear. On the other hand, once you get a license, you can share the commission on any property you buy, saving half the amount of commission. Depending on the price of the property, this can add up to big savings.

Home-Buying Strategy No. 11: Buy Wholesale

People who are willing "shop until they drop" to get the best deal on clothes or a television still pay retail prices for their home—even though that home costs a thousand times more than the most expensive pair of shoes. This is foolish. Instead of paying retail prices for real estate, buy direct from the owner—the real estate equivalent of "wholesale."

In the housing market, wholesale homes are referred to as "For Sale by Owners" (FSBOs in the trade). Certainly, not all FSBOs are good buys. In fact, many people sell their homes themselves to save the commission and put more money in their own pocket. These people frequently overprice their homes at the beginning. The key is to spot the motivated sellers—for example, sellers who have had their homes on the market for many months and have become frustrated. These are the types of sellers who will end up slashing their prices just so that they can get out of the property.

There are many other reasons why people may be motivated to sell their homes. When they are, it is much easier to get a bargain. This is similar to a retailer who needs cash quick and runs an "everything on sale" event. Here are some motivations to watch for:

- ★ People who have been transferred to a new job and have to move by a deadline
- ★ Foreclosure situations
- ★ Divorces
- ★ Estate sales
- ★ Investors who own property and are tired of management
- ★ Tax sales
- ★ Bankruptcy sales

These are just some of the opportunities available for buying wholesale. Each can be a source for a good buy on a single home or a viable niche for a business. In fact, we know of people who have made a living specializing in just one of these areas.

PROTECT YOUR REAL ESTATE INVESTMENT

Buying your home is only the first step in the process. Once you have found the home you want, you must take steps to safeguard your valuable investment.

Home-Buying Strategy No. 12: Don't Overpay Because of an Emotional Investment

It's a bad day when you (or your spouse) fall in love with a property and decide that you simply *have to* have it. When situations like this develop, try to keep your emotions under control; step back and look at the deal from a distance. Emotional attachment (for whatever reason) *costs you money.*

Home-Buying Strategy No. 13: Use the Contract to Your Advantage

Another strategy to counter the effects of the "buying bug" is to make your contract contingent on your getting an appraisal for at least the amount of the purchase price. By getting your own appraisal, you are bringing in a third-party expert who will tell you if you are overpaying. You may still want to go ahead with the deal, but taking this important step may keep you from making a big mistake.

Home-Buying Strategy No. 14: Rent to Own

If you can't come up with the down payment for a home or if you can't qualify for a mortgage, try to get an option to buy on a home that you can rent. Negotiate with the owner. Try to convince him or her to let some of the rent you pay be credited toward a future down payment if you decide to purchase the property.

Options to purchase are a lot more common than you might think, and they can be a good way to build future value, even if you are still forced to rent for the time being. Once the credited portion of your rent equals the down payment required to qualify for a loan, you can (but don't have to) exercise your option to buy the property. Additionally, lenders will look more favorably upon buyers who have a solid record of paying the rent on time, and who are trying to buy the home that they have been living in for a year or more.

Home-Buying Strategy No. 15: Be Builder-Wary

We hate to dampen anyone's enthusiasm for buying a new home. At the same time, we have to warn you to keep your eyes open. Brand-new homes come with particular reasons for caution.

When you are looking at a builder's model home, you must understand that what you see there is the *best possible version* of what you'll get. The reality is likely to be something less than this vision of perfection.

There are all kinds of builders out there. There are honest builders who will go overboard to make sure you get everything you want. There are dishonest ones, too. And there's a third group that you also have to watch out for: builders who are stretched too thin financially and can't finish what they've started. To guard against this possibility, cover yourself with a good contract that spells out in detail exactly what you are going to get when everything is built, and don't forget to include deadlines for completion of various aspects of the home.

We have seen too many people who have been stuck when builders overcommitted and could not meet their delivery dates. These buyers had to live with parents and friends while they waited for their homes to be finished. Consider putting a performance penalty in your builder's contract. After a reasonable grace period, the builder starts *paying you* for every day he or she delivers the home late. An alternative to a penalty is a performance bonus if the builder finishes on time. This clause is positive reinforcement and can get you the best attention. Either way, consult with your attorney. He or she can serve as your "front man" in the negotiation, so that you can maintain a good, positive relationship with your builder.

New homes in larger developments can introduce special problems. If you are buying in the early stages of a development project, *do everything you can* to check out the developer and his or her track record. If the developer runs into financial problems, you and your neighbors could end up with unfinished streets, pools, golf courses, or clubhouses.

To check out builders and developers, go to the local homebuilder's association in your area. Additionally, you can check for complaints with the local Better Business Bureau and do an online search for articles on the builder or developer.

Home-Buying Strategy No. 16: Understand Your Survey

When you get your financing, your lender will almost certainly require a survey of the property you are buying. If it doesn't, make sure you order one for yourself. In either case, *review the survey*. The survey basically says who owns what, so it's not something you can afford to make a mistake on. Don't count on the lender to do the review; we have seen lender-accepted surveys with numerous encroachment problems that no one discovered until years later.

Most people never even meet their surveyor, and that's not smart. You paid good money for this expert (yes, the bank makes you pay for it), so make a point of talking to him or her one-on-one. Don't be afraid to ask the surveyor if he or she sees any potential problems.

Make sure you understand the results of your survey so that you can head off any problems down the line. We once bought a piece of property that had a driveway extending onto the neighbor's property. That little item never came up in the first survey. Fortunately, we had great neighbors, and there was no problem—but there *could* have been.

Home-Buying Strategy No. 17: Understand Your Title

Your *title* is the evidence of your legal right to your property. You can buy something called *title insurance* that supposedly limits your exposure to a "clouded" (i.e., disputed) title.

Unfortunately, title insurance isn't what most people think it is. In fact, it *doesn't* insure your ownership against all title problems; it insures your ownership only against title problems for which the title company has not listed an exception. And guess what? The title company will list every exception it can possibly think of. If you accept a policy with all of the exceptions in place, it will be *your* problem if one of them arises.

Make the title company delete any exceptions you don't like. If it won't do that, shop for another title company. By the way: while you are shopping, make sure you are dealing with a large, reputable company, not just anyone who will write a policy. Title insurance won't do you any good if the company has gone out of business when you need to make a claim.

Title exceptions are becoming a common part of the buying process. Do not rely on your real estate agent to help you in this area, since it is very rare for real estate agents to read these. The reason? They are not trained to do so, and in most states, the buyer will need a lawyer to render an opinion on one. Please read your policy carefully, and make sure you understand what the policy covers. If you don't, ask your lawyer for help.

Home-Buying Strategy No. 18: Get It in Writing

When purchasing a home, you will encounter a blizzard of paperwork, including a contract that may be very confusing. Don't let your eyes glaze over—and don't sign anything you don't understand. And remember that if someone promises you something, it doesn't count until you get it in writing.

Let's take a look at some of the key areas where "getting it in writing" is crucial.

Contingent on Financing

Very few people can pay all cash for a home. Unless you are one of these people, make sure your contract specifically states that your offer is contingent upon your getting financing for the home. Without that language, the seller can try to force you to close on the contract, and can sue you personally if you are unable to obtain financing. Protect yourself and your family with this simple clause.

The best way to phrase your contract is to make it "subject to the buyer securing financing on terms acceptable to him in his sole discretion." Without this specific language, you might be forced to accept financing terms that you can't afford or that are otherwise inappropriate for your circumstances.

Contingent on Appraisal

If a broker isn't representing you, make sure you get your own appraisal on the property. Also, make sure that the contract is contingent on the appraisal's coming in at an amount equal to or greater than the purchase price.

If the buyer, or anyone else, shows you an appraisal that was already done on the property, do not assume that it's correct or still current. We're not suggesting fraud, but many times we've seen appraisals on a particular property differ by 15 percent or more. On commercial properties, we've seen disparities that run into the millions of dollars.

Home-Buying Strategy No. 19: Realize That Profit Is in the Buying

We started this list of home-buying strategies with the age-old tenet about the importance of location. We'll end it with another long-standing rule.

You make your biggest profit on a property when *you* buy it. In other words, if you are careful to structure a good deal on the front end, you are likely to sell with a good profit. This means that the price you pay for any property will probably determine how successful you are in selling the home for a profit down the line.

You may be lucky and get added appreciation for other reasons, but that's just icing on the cake. Focus on structuring a good deal from the beginning, and chances are you will be the richer for it later. If you don't feel comfortable with the price going in, then we recommend that you not buy the property. Go find a deal that you *are* comfortable with.

YOUR MISSION TO WEALTH TO-DO LIST

1. RESOLVE TO OWN YOUR OWN HOME AS SOON AS POSSIBLE. There is simply no more important milestone on the path to financial freedom. The financial benefits can be enormous, and the psychological benefits may be even more important. (They don't call home ownership "the American Dream" for nothing.)

2. DO YOUR HOMEWORK. Study the options that your budget allows. Find the right town, and then find the right neighborhood *within* that town. (Neighborhoods can vary greatly, even in a "great town.") Make sure your proposed house is in the right school district. Easy access to a reliable public transportation system can make a big difference, too. Remember, the three most important things in real estate are *location, location,* and *location.*

3. GET THE HELP YOU NEED. Get in touch with the local real estate brokerage community. Consider using a buyer's broker. Involve your lawyer whenever there are legal issues on the table. A building inspector can protect you from all kinds of structural problems, including those that aren't visible to the naked eye. Make sure to be on hand to meet and talk with your surveyor when it comes time to figure out the exact borders of the property—he or she can often tell you a lot about your property.

4. REMEMBER THAT THE PROFIT IS IN THE BUYING. In other words, the deal that you strike in the first place goes a long way toward determining how much money you'll make in the long run. Buy with your *head*, not your heart. Buy wholesale, if possible. Get the best possible mortgage, with the most flexibility in terms of prepayments and refinancings.

5. IF YOU MAKE REAL ESTATE YOUR BUSINESS, DO EVEN MORE HOMEWORK. Yes, there's money to be made in real estate, but there's also money to be lost in real estate. Read the right books. (Ilyce Glink's *100 Questions Every First-Time Home Buyer Should Ask* is good for residential real estate; *The Real Estate Game*, by Harvard's William Poorvu, covers commercial real estate.) Take courses at your local community college. Get involved with local real estate investors' groups. Remember that real estate is particularly prone to the boom-and-bust cycle, and that your goal is to *buy at the bottom*, if possible.

★ ★ ★

CHAPTER 9

Cars: How to Drive a Real Bargain

Let us never negotiate out of fear. But let us never fear to negotiate.

—John Fitzgerald Kennedy

With the exception of your home, the car you drive is one of the biggest purchases you make. In fact, if you add up the value of all of the cars you will purchase over the course of your lifetime, and if you own more than one car and trade them in regularly, transportation may actually cost you *more* than housing.

Each year, more than 25 million people open up their wallets to buy a new or used car. Many of them have never stopped to think about how they might save money in the process. But if you add up the potential savings over a lifetime of car purchases, you'll see that it's a substantial sum. You're far better off putting this money in your own nest egg, rather than handing it over to car dealerships and banks.

America's love for the automobile isn't showing signs of fading, even as gasoline prices continue on their inevitable march upward. We *love* to drive. Our culture is all about freedom and mobility and movement. Even if it weren't, the unavailability or inadequacy of public transportation pushes us toward owning a car—or cars.

As a rule, when young buyers walk into a showroom, they are mainly interested in how much money they're going to have to put down and the size of their monthly payment. If the truth be told, many older buyers also use the same analysis, or lack of analysis. They focus on the demands of the present, without paying enough attention to the fact that what they buy may have a powerful impact on how they ultimately live.

Car-Buying Strategy No. 1: Do Your Homework and Save Big Bucks

We've made this point regularly in previous chapters: If you're an educated consumer, you have a much better chance of saving real money when you buy your car, new or used. And the best education you can get, when buying your car, is to *shop and compare*. Yes, this is time consuming. But saving 3 percent on a $20,000 car is a $600 savings on the front end, plus the additional savings you realize on reduced interest costs and lower sales and excise taxes.

Comparison shopping for a car is a lot easier than it was a decade ago. The Internet has truly transformed the car-buying process, particularly for those who know how to use the data they collect. All major car manufacturers have Web sites, and while they don't post many of the discounts that may be available, you can learn a lot. Brochures and product information can be found in abundance, ready for downloading. By using the Web, you can save wear and tear on your current car, not to mention a whole lot of time, aggravation, and gas money driving from dealer to dealer.

Consumerreports.org is a great place to start. It offers a great deal of free information, and it also has two paid services that will prepare you well for negotiations with your neighborhood car dealer. For $12, you can get a 10- to 20-page report on any car you want; this report tells you the *real* numbers to deal on, like the dealer's invoice price (what the dealer paid) and the manufacturer's suggested retail price (MSRP) (what the dealer wants you to pay), plus safety ratings, prices for options, rebates available, and tips on getting the best deal. For unlimited reports, there is a three-month service for $39.

> *The sleeping fox catches no poultry.*
>
> —Benjamin Franklin

Another good tactic is to consult a copy of Edmunds Car Prices Buyer's Guide (try your local library, or check online at Edmunds.com). This resource will give you both the wholesale and the retail price of almost every car on the market today. The guide also tells you the approximate markups for other features dealers tack on. Knowing the dealer's markup allows you to reduce the sticker price by the appropriate percentage, while establishing a price that you are willing to pay for the car. This can create a win-win situation, in which the dealer makes some money but does not gouge you in the process.

OK, now you know approximately what you should pay for your car. There's another important piece to your comparison shopping: *looking for the best financing rates.* Since the dealer is going to try to persuade you to take one of its financing packages (as described later), you need to walk in already knowing your alternatives, at least in a preliminary way. You'll get another chance later, but you want to be in a position to know, on the spot, whether the dealer is actually offering you a good deal.

While most of the major automobile manufacturers have attractive interest rates and loan packages (especially when they get desperate to move aging products off their lots), there are many places where you can get at least 1/2 percent lower interest by shopping for a loan. Credit unions are a good place to start. Because they are member-based organizations, they provide low-cost loans to their members. Call around and see if you can join any of your local credit unions. Have that best real-world rate in your head *before* you approach a dealership.

Car-Buying Strategy No. 2: Save the Most on Every Car You Buy

Everybody loves to buy a new car when he or she has the opportunity, but a new car certainly isn't the cheapest. The moment you drive the car off the lot, it loses approximately *30 percent* of its value because of the depreciation that is allowed for the dealer's initial markup. If you had to sell that car immediately, you would take a bath on the transaction.

Given this backdrop, from a purely financial standpoint, the best way to buy a car is to shop for a one- or two-year-old car. Some of the best buys are in luxury cars, since their owners trade them in frequently, thereby creating a glut in this particular segment of the used-car market.

The availability of these cars has also increased because of the proliferation of two-year lease programs. The lessee turns in the car at the end of the lease, and the dealer then puts it up for sale. Sometimes these prices are lower than the lessee could have purchased the car for under the lease plan. No, it doesn't make sense—but that doesn't mean that *you* shouldn't take advantage of the opportunity.

Car-Buying Strategy No. 3: Buy at the Best Time and Save

We always wondered if you really could save money if you bought a car at certain times of the year. So we spent some time with a real industry insider (a successful auto broker) to get the inside story. The answer? *Yes, you can,* if you know how the game works.

The key to picking the best time, according to our friend, is to look for slow periods in overall car sales. If the economy is down, car deals will get better. Even spikes in gasoline prices can lower the cost of a car, as many potential buyers will worry themselves into not buying.

> *Delay is preferable to error.*
> —Thomas Jefferson

There are other good "buy days" as well:

- ★ *The two weeks before and after Christmas.* Who wants to buy a car at Christmas? You might.
- ★ *Right after a hurricane, snowstorm, or other bad weather.* We don't want to promote disaster buying, but you'll be helping to boost the economy while getting yourself a deal.
- ★ *When new models are introduced.* All around this period, promotions on both new and used cars are at a peak.

Car-Buying Strategy No. 4: Be a Smart Negotiator

Most people dread car negotiations. Actually, if you've done the homework we just recommended, the negotiations for your new car ought to be pretty straightforward. You already know the dealer's profit margins—both on the car itself and on the options you might be interested in—and you already have a sense of how much profit you think the dealer should make on your purchase. Be clear about your position, and stick to it. The worst that will happen is that the dealer won't agree to your terms. Fine; make a date at another nearby dealership and go talk to that dealer.

Don't get emotional. Don't get stampeded. There's no rush. You're the one with the money, so *you hold the cards*. If the dealer gets pushy, tell him or her that you don't appreciate that tactic. If the dealer gets pushy again, politely end the conversation and leave.

If you start closing in on a deal, remember that dealer-installed equipment is another expensive add-on. Yes, those fancy chrome wheels look great. But do you really *need* them? Or can you live with the standard wheels and save your money for smarter purchases or investments? (If you *have* to have those fancy rims, buy them down the street from an aftermarket parts store. They'll be much cheaper.) Is the TV for the backseat passengers important if you normally don't have backseat passengers? If the TV in the backseat is already installed, ask how much less you'd pay for the same car without the TV. Will the dealer take it out and give you a cash credit?

Let's assume that things go well, and that you agree on a price for the car you want with (only) the options you want. *Don't relax;* you're not done negotiating yet. Now you have to go to contract, and almost without exception, the dealer will try to make more money on you in the contract phase.

In what way? Well, dealer preparation charges are one of the most common "extras" a dealer tries to pass on. This is the fee the dealer charges you for getting your car ready for sale. In most cases, except for needing to be washed, your car was probably ready when it arrived at the dealership, so this fee is nothing but pure profit for the dealer. Sometimes you can get the "dealer prep" charge waived, sometimes you can get a portion

Wars are not won by defensive tactics.

—George S. Patton

144

waived, and other times you will simply have to pay it in full. But if you don't *ask* the dealer to waive or reduce it, you will pay the full price for sure.

Even if the dealer won't waive the charge, argue the point. You can use it as a bargaining chip on your next point of negotiation. (Rest assured that there will be more points to negotiate!) Remind the dealer that you gave in on the dealer prep charge, so she or he needs to give a little this time.

Rustproofing may be your next battle line. You just bought a car with all the latest technological advances, and yet somehow the manufacturer neglected to rustproof the bottom of your car. Wonder why? Profit, of course. If the dealer has already rustproofed the car and just added the cost onto the sticker price, it is nego- tiable, so speak up. All the rustproofing amounts to is a little spray that you could have put on much more cheaply yourself. If the dealer hasn't done it, waive the service and get it done somewhere else. Or do it yourself and save even more money.

Or don't do it *at all.* Keep in mind that metallurgy has improved dramatically in the last two decades, and cars don't rust out nearly as fast as they used to—even without that extra dose of rustproof- ing that the dealer is trying to sell you. Ask the dealer how long the car is warranted against body rust-through. Is that long enough for your needs?

Car-Buying Strategy No. 5: Don't Jump at Those So-Called Extended Warranties

We like the new-car warranties being offered by almost all the auto- mobile manufacturers. Currently, they are running from three to five years, with 40,000 to 50,000 miles bumper-to-bumper protection. But almost all dealers will try to sell you add-on warranties. These plans sound like they are an *additional* three to five years, but, in fact, most of them also count the period during which you are already covered by the original manufacturer's warranty.

It gets very expensive to buy the add-on coverage at the time you buy your car. Before you buy the extended warranty, carefully consider how long you plan to keep the car. Consider the added cost the dealer proposes to charge you for the actual number of *additional years* of protection. And finally, ask if this coverage will be available at a later date. In most cases, it will be, and deferring the decision until later will give you more time to figure out whether you like the car and want to keep it long term.

One additional note on this point: If you buy extended warranties, *keep the paperwork handy.* It's easy to lose track of what you bought and how long it extends. If the GM dealer sells you a third-party extended warranty when you buy the car (which isn't unusual), you're likely to get a solicitation from GM several years down the road, offering an extended warranty as the GM warranty approaches expiration. You need to know what coverage you already have in place, and for how much longer.

Car-Buying Strategy No. 6: Understand the Rules of Auto Finance

Don't relax; you're still not done negotiating. Now you have to *finance* the car, and this is where many dealers make a big part of their profit.

Your next hour or so at the dealer will be spent with the business manager (or the "finance manager," as some are called). Even if you are prepared and inclined to pay cash, you still have to meet this person. Why? Because the dealer wants to see if it can change your mind and get you to take out a loan from the dealer instead.

Today, dealers have many financing choices to offer you. First, they will run your credit report to get your credit score and see which of their financing programs you qualify for. If you have worked on improving your credit rating, as explained in earlier chapters, you will now reap the rewards by getting a lower rate offered to you. And, of course, a lower rate is good, but remember the key question: *good compared to what?*

At this point in the buying process, it is a "lower" rate only compared to the other rates the dealer is offering. Could you get a lower rate somewhere else? Well, if you've done your homework, you'll know what's available. (Remember, checking on car financing *before* you visited the dealer was part of your research.) Now, sitting in the business manager's office, you have some quotes from the real world, which means that you may have some real ammo to use in your negotiations.

If your quotes are lower, show them to the business manager and offer to let him or her beat the price if he or she can. In most cases, you will quickly see that the first quote the business manager gave you wasn't the best. Does that mean that you have to accept the next offer? Of course not, if you're not satisfied. Just write it down, then tell the business manager that you're going to check a few other places, and you will let her or him know which source of financing you want to use.

Of course, you won't get to drive your car off the lot until you get it financed, but checking other places for a better rate is *always* the smart way to go. And demonstrating that you have other options, and that you intend to explore them, may be the best way to bring the dealer's price down.

Car-Buying Strategy No. 7: Put Less Down If Interest Rates Are Low

We've made this point before, but we'll make it again. When it comes to borrowing money, ask yourself whether you can make more interest (or return on your money) than you will have to pay to borrow the money. If you can, borrow more. If you can't, put more money down.

Keep in mind that market conditions can change quickly. For example, in a high-interest-rate environment, you might be able to lock up high-quality bonds (or a bond fund) yielding more than 5 percent. But if interest rates fall (which is usually a positive for the stock market), the yield on bonds and CDs will fall with it. So you need to take this into account when making the decision on financing your car loan.

Car-Buying Strategy No. 8: Pick the Right Length of Loan

"Buying the payment" has become common in the world of car buying. This means that you stretch out the term of the loan longer and get the payments down to a level that you're comfortable with. This is a *bad* strategy. It's why many people can't get out of debt. The longer the term of your loan, the greater the percentage of each early payment that goes solely to interest, not to paying off the principal balance of your loan.

Aside from your own budget, there are other reasons not to "buy the payment." For example, your new car depreciates fastest in the first two years that you own it. As a result, you may find that you owe more than the car is actually worth. (This is called getting "upside down" on your car loan.) When that happens, either you'll have to keep the car longer than you want to or you'll have to come up with cash to pay the difference if you want to sell or trade it.

To avoid this financing trap, try to limit your car loan to a 36-month term, which more closely approximates your car's depreciation schedule.

Car-Buying Strategy No. 9: Learn the Truth about Credit Life Insurance

Most lenders offer you something called "credit life insurance" when you get a car loan. This is simply a form of term insurance that will pay off your car loan should you die.

While term insurance is a good idea, these credit life policies cover a decreasing loan balance, even though you make a constant payment. In other words, should you die, your loan will be paid off. If you die right after you buy the car, the $20,000 loan would be fully reimbursed. However, if you died right before making your final payment, then only the last payment would be reimbursed.

Instead of this kind of credit life insurance, get your own term insurance for the full value of the loan. You will pay almost the same amount, but should you die, your heirs would get the full $20,000, no matter when you are "taken out of the picture" (the euphemism many insurance agents use to avoid using the word *die*).

Car-Buying Strategy No. 10: Sell Your Old Car Yourself

Last but not least, what about the car you plan to get *rid* of when you purchase your new car? Yes, selling your own car is a hassle. But if you don't sell your car yourself, your laziness can cost you dearly.

You don't believe us? Ask the dealer for his or her price with trade-in and without, and you'll learn instantly how little you are really getting for your car. The reason is that the dealer is offering you the *wholesale* price for your car. This is the price the dealer knows he or she can get without doing anything more than running your car through the auctions to sell it.

Action may not always bring happiness; but there is no happiness without action.

—Benjamin Disraeli

If your car is in great condition, the dealer may try to sell it on the used-car lot. But if the dealer can't move it quickly at retail, she or he will dump it wholesale.

To get the most for your money, sell your car yourself, retail. Spend a little money detailing the car and get it looking good, then offer it for sale. Check out Web sites like eBaymotors.com and Autotrader.com, which allow you to buy or sell cars online. These sites are also useful for comparison shopping and pricing.

If you do sell your car yourself, check with your state title agency to make sure you know *exactly how to do it correctly*. While the transfer process is simple, you need to know what to do to avoid the kind of glitch that keeps you on record as the owner. Keep your own insurance going on your car until you are absolutely sure that your loan has been paid off and the transfer is complete.

YOUR MISSION TO WEALTH TO-DO LIST

1. **FIGURE OUT WHAT THAT CAR, AND ITS OPTIONS, IS WORTH.** Before you look for your car, research it online at www.Consumerreports.org, www.Edmunds.com,

or www.Autotrader.com. There's an absolute wealth of information available to you—much of it at no charge. Even the modest fees that these resources may charge you are likely to be well worth it.

2. FIGURE OUT WHAT YOU SHOULD PAY FOR THAT AUTO LOAN. Check local credit unions and online at www. LendingTree.com *before* you go to a dealer, so that you have a way of assessing the loan that the dealer offers you. Remember that you strike the deal on the car first, then you have the opportunity to strike a deal *elsewhere* for the loan. Let the dealer know that you will definitely go with the best deal.

3. GUARD AGAINST ADD-ONS. Don't fall in love with those rims. Don't take the extended warranty without some close scrutiny. Don't buy credit life insurance. Think of it this way: If you went to the supermarket, you wouldn't let the clerks put extra stuff in your cart. Don't let that happen at the dealership, at any stage in the negotiations.

4. SELL THAT CLUNKER YOURSELF. No, there's nothing much fun about selling your used car—except, of course, that you get to put the extra money you'll make into your bank account, where it will do good things for you for many years to come.

★ ★ ★

PART 3

Executing
the Mission

The following chapters are some of the most important in determining how successful you will be in securing your financial future. Part 3 starts by showing you how to create a wealth-building plan and continues with a chapter that reveals concrete ways to implement your investment plan. Also included are chapters on building your retirement nest egg, minimizing your taxes (legally, of course), and building a fund for your child's education.

We wrap up this part with ideas on building a millionaire legacy and a practical chapter on the advantages of starting and running your own business—a wealth-building technique that we wholeheartedly endorse.

These eight chapters form the nucleus of our wealth-building plan. They will give you the tools and techniques you will need to execute the mission.

★ ★ ★

CHAPTER 10

Create a Wealth-Building Investment Plan

The control of a large force is the same principle as the control of a few men.

—Sun Tzu

Investing is a scary proposition for most people. In many cases, that's because they have had no formal training in making investment decisions, and they are under the impression that they always have to be right. That's not true, of course. (Nobody's *always* right, especially in the investing arena.) But because of their lack of financial education and their resulting lack of confidence, novice investors often run for the hills (or to the nearest bank to buy a certificate of deposit) at the first sign of trouble.

One of the keys to investing is understanding that *investing is a lifetime proposition.* Since you will be investing all your life, the sooner you start learning about the process, the better off you'll be, and the more money you'll make. Fortunately, you don't have to learn it all at once. Learn a little bit each year, and restrict your investing to the fields and instruments that you've already become comfortable with. When you gain and use knowledge this way, you won't have to rely on what other people think is right. Instead, you'll *know* what is right, because you will have learned it yourself. It's like driving your car along a route that you figured out yourself. You *know* this particular way to get from Point A to Point B. (You figured it out yourself.) You don't need help making your journey.

A related (and reassuring) principle of investing is that most of what you learn will be "scalable." This simply means that the disciplines you learn while you're managing a small amount of money will be the same ones you will use to manage a much larger sum. So taking the time to learn the fundamentals *thoroughly, at the outset,* is a very, very wise investment of your time. It will continue to pay off when your funds are bigger and the stakes are higher.

Keep in mind, too, that you can take as many "practice swings" as you want. When people use our financial software, for example, we teach them to "paper trade" first, before they put real money at risk.

> *Take calculated risks.*
> *That is quite different*
> *from being rash.*
> —George S. Patton

We certainly can't teach you everything about investing in a few pages. But we *can* expose you to a range of different instruments and strategies, so that you can follow up and learn more about each of them.

That is the essence of what we are hoping to achieve in this chapter.

Investment Strategy No. 1: Create the "Best" Investment for Financial Freedom

Since there are so many ways to invest your money, it might seem that you should find the best one and start investing there. That's a good idea, except that unfortunately there's no one "best way" to invest. Your task, therefore, is to find the investment that best fits your temperament, understanding, and long-term goals.

Let's look at some specifics. One of the best investment categories is real estate. In previous chapters, we discussed the importance of buying a home. Perhaps you've already learned enough about real estate to want to make it the focal point of your investment program. Perhaps your good experience with your home is tempting you to buy another piece of property for investment purposes.

If so, we caution you to move slowly. We have known many people who've been bitten by the real estate bug, only to find out that to be successful in dealing with tenants and rental property management requires a certain personality. You won't know this until you actually live through the ups and downs of property management. You certainly don't want to make the discovery *after* you've bought several properties, so once again, we highly recommend that you proceed with caution.

How about the stock market? Stock market investing is not necessarily the road to Easy Street, either. It's gratifying to be invested in the market when it's moving up, but what goes up almost always comes down. Markets change from day to day, and from week to week. The 1990s saw the longest-running bull market in history. It seemed as if everyone was making money. Unfortunately, when the party ended with the tech bust of 2000, many people *lost* a lot of money, too.

Many investors had trouble with the bear market that followed. It takes nerves of steel to "play" the market during very volatile times. Those who can't handle the stress wind up selling when they should be buying, and vice versa.

So if there's no one best answer, what do you do? We suggest that you start by memorizing the first rule of investing: Don't put all your eggs in one basket. If you follow this basic concept, you will necessarily expose yourself to different types of investments, and

There are always risks, but I am used to risks.

—Donald Rumsfeld

this will help you to discover your own method. While you're spreading your risk (a good idea in and of itself), you will also be getting familiar with different types of investments.

Your goal should be to diversify your holdings *across* different investment arenas, and also *within* them. If you're buying stocks, for example, buy stocks in different sectors of the market. Normally, the market moves in cycles, and pieces of the market move counter to other pieces. Learning about sectors and cycles helps you spread your risk, so that you are less likely to get killed when different parts of the stock market suffer downturns.

Mutual funds are another useful tool. Investing in mutual funds and exchange-traded funds (ETFs) instead of individual stocks gives you instant diversification, overseen by professional managers. ETFs are only a couple of years old as an investment product, but they have already attracted lots of positive attention. Like mutual funds, they offer diversity in specific areas, like energy, but offer the advantage of lower management fees and operational costs.

The largest and most actively traded ETFs are the ones on the major indexes: the Nasdaq 100 (QQQQ), the Dow Jones Industrial Average (DIA), and the S&P 500 (SPY). These ETFs allow you to buy an entire basket of stocks as if you were buying only one stock. For example, the SPY ETF represents all the stocks in the Standard & Poor's 500. By buying even one share, you get the diversification of 500 stocks.

No, we're not pushing ETFs as the "best" investment. Remember, our larger point here is the importance of diversification. Don't just buy real estate; buy other assets to complement your real estate portfolio. When buying stocks, take advantage of existing vehicles for diversification. Mutual funds are one; ETFs are another. *Don't put all your eggs in one basket.*

OUR TOP INVESTMENT STRATEGIES

The following strategies will help you to start your own investment program. Some of them will be familiar to you; others will not. One thing we always recommend is that you review the list frequently and make revisions to it every so often. It is amazing how much people forget, over time. Having these reminders can be a big help.

As your list of favorite strategies grows, you will wind up with your own investing "black book." (We'll return to this concept later in the chapter.) We suggest that you read through this chapter once quickly, then come back and go through each strategy slowly. Over time, you should adopt as many of these strategies as you can and make them positive habits in your investing life.

As we mentioned in Chapter 8, "Own Your Own Home," you make your best profit *when you buy*. The same holds true for other forms of investing. Nothing can substitute for doing your homework. In other words, research a stock thoroughly *before* you buy it. There's simply no good alternative. If you're buying a stock based simply on the latest hot tip, you might just as well be putting your money on black at the roulette wheel. [In fact, your 50/50 odds at the roulette table (black versus red) are probably *better* than your odds when you plunge in the stock market.]

Investment Strategy No. 2: Pay Off Your High-Interest Credit Cards

Let's start at the beginning, which involves going back to a point made in previous chapters. There's no investment that you can make that is as productive as *paying off your credit cards*. Simply put, this is one of the best things you can do with your money.

Once again, if you have credit card balances, and you are paying 16 to 21 percent in interest on those balances, every dollar you can put toward reducing that debt is the same as earning 16 to 21 percent on that same dollar. In addition, your return is guaranteed, because you have reduced the debt and saved all of the interest you would have paid. Not many things on Wall Street are guaranteed. This is one *sure way* to get a great return on your money.

You'll never find a better investment than credit card debt reduction, so do this before you make any other investment. Not only will you make a high guaranteed return, but you will relieve the stress that heavy debt brings and improve your personal monthly cash flow. Do it first. Do it *now*.

Investment Strategy No. 3: Follow the Trend

Asset classes (those things in which you will make your investments) tend to follow trend lines. Sometimes they go up, sometimes they go down, and sometimes they move sideways. It has been said, "The trend is your friend." This means that if you adjust your investing according to the direction of the trend, you will achieve a higher probability of success.

> It is best not to swap
> horses in mid-stream.
> —Abraham Lincoln

A good starting rule for putting money in the stock market, for example, is to wait until the three major indexes (the Dow, S&P 500, and Nasdaq) are above their long-term "moving average" of 200 days. The moving average for each index is a number plotted on a chart showing the closing value for the day. By averaging the numbers for the previous 200 days and plotting that average on the graph, you get a 200-day moving average, which provides a good picture of how the market is trending.

Historically, the 200-day moving average has been a significant number that helps investors determine the overall trend of the stock market. If the indices are above that average line, this indicates that the market may be moving higher. If they are below the line, then the overall market is not performing well, and investments are generally down. See the example below.

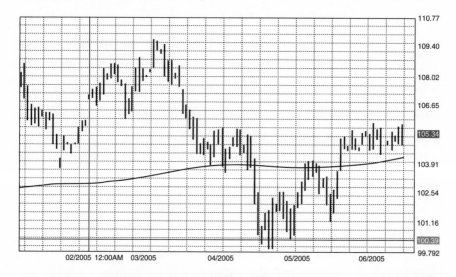

The 200-day moving average is represented by the line in the above chart. As the price of the Dow Jones Industrial Average moves above this line, it is a positive trend for the market. (*Courtesy of PremiereTrade™AI*)

There are also other moving averages that traders and active investors follow to give them market indications. The 50-day moving average, for example, looks at a shorter time span. Investors who follow this indicator tend to be more active, in the sense of moving in and out of the market on short notice. Conservative investors can also learn to use the shorter moving average to pull their money out of the general market sooner, and thereby be quicker to move into money markets that entail very low risk.

Investment Strategy No. 4: Learn the Best Time to Sell

Jumping out of a winning investment too soon is always frustrating. You tend to kick yourself over and over. You were *right* in your research and *right* in your purchase—and then you sold too soon. But stop kicking yourself. There is also a very important principle that we'd like to introduce you to, if you don't know it already: "Never be afraid to take a profit."

The simple fact is that if all you ever did was take small but quick profits, your annualized returns would be huge, and you would be a very happy investor overall. On the other hand, you don't want to let go of a true winner too quickly. We think the way to split the difference is to let your profits run, but *after you've met your objectives, use stop loss orders, or stops, to keep yourself from falling back in the red.*

What's a stop loss order? It's an instruction to your broker (or an order that you set on an online brokerage account) that if a stock falls back to a certain price level, it should be sold automatically. A good rule of thumb on a stock you like is to allow for a "retracement" of one-half of the gain as the stock moves up. In other words, if you buy the stock at $1, and it goes up to $2, you set your stop loss order at $1.50. By allowing for some retracement (that is, the zone between $2.00 and $1.50), you'll give the stock some room for downward correction but also give it a chance to rebound and resume its upward path.

Another investment tool used by more active traders is to follow the upward movement of a stock with trailing stops, based on support and resistance points. As noted earlier, a stop is an order to sell your stock at a predetermined price. It's most often used as a form of protection—either to lock in a gain or to decrease losses.

The *trailing stop* is simply a stop that moves as your stock's price moves. For an example, you might decide that you want to unload a stock if it ever drops 5 percent. In that case, your trailing stop rises along with the stock price. Suppose your $1 per share stock rises to $3 and then stalls. If you've set a trailing stop of 5 percent on that stock, it will be sold automatically if the price drops to $2.85 (5 percent less than $3 per share). If the price keeps rising but then stalls at $4, the stock will be sold automatically if it falls to $3.80 (5 percent less than $4 per share).

If a stock price breaks a *support point* (i.e., if it falls below a key price), there is usually a reason for the slide—for example, bad news about the stock. Selling out at this point preserves your gain and gives you some "calm time" to rethink your position.

Resistance points are pretty much polar opposites of support points. They are a selling trigger on the upside. In other words, they are predetermined price points at which your investment will automatically be sold. These may be based on past experience (for example, the percentage gain at which the stock has stopped climbing in the past) or on larger market indicators that suggest that a pause is in the wings. You can learn to calculate these key points yourself, or you can use software that rapidly does it for you.

THREE INDISPENSABLE RULES FOR MAKING ANY INVESTMENT

Investment Strategy No. 5: Never Confuse Your Investments with Your Political Feelings

Some people believe in investing in companies that promote a particular cause. We don't. Don't mix the two. If you are committed to a particular cause, donate your profits to that cause at some later date. Think of it this way: Once you have made money by sticking to sound investing principles, you will be in a better position to donate more to your favorite charity.

Investment Strategy No. 6: If It Sounds Too Good to Be True, It Is

We know you've heard this before (the U.S. Postal Service says it all the time), but it bears repeating. One of the biggest problems we encounter with new investors is unrealistic expectations. Remember, there's no shortcut to Easy Street. If someone offers you a rate of return that's substantially higher than the return on the general market, then either you're dealing with a crook or there's higher risk associated with that investment. This is a fact that you can take to the bank. Don't be taken in by the latest "hot deal."

Investment Strategy No. 7: Don't Fall in Love with Your Investments

People buy stock in companies for a lot of different reasons. Peter Lynch, one of the world's most successful money managers, suggests buying stocks in companies whose products you know and like. That's all well and good. (It takes advantage of your expertise as a consumer.) But there is a place to draw the line, and that's when a company starts to underperform. Don't ever stay with a company simply because you like its products, its commercials, its catalogs, or whatever. If its stock is not performing well, it is time to get out.

Investment Strategy No. 8: Narrow Your Field of Stocks or Specialize

Between the individual stocks and all the mutual funds that are available for purchase out there, there are simply too many options to be followed by an individual investor. To become a successful investor, therefore, you will need to either narrow your possibilities using screening techniques or decide to specialize in a particular area of the market.

A good choice is to specialize in a field you know well. This is a well-loved strategy of investing great Warren Buffett, as well as many other successful investors. The idea is that you will have the most luck if you invest in those areas with which you are most familiar. For example, a doctor might become an expert in pharmaceutical companies. The doctor could use his medical knowledge to determine whether a new drug has the potential to become a blockbuster, boosting corporate profits and lifting the price of the stock.

By sticking to those areas you know best, you protect yourself from investing in fads that you don't understand. For example, Buffett—a self-described technophobe—was chided for not jumping on the Internet bandwagon in the 1990s. Instead, he stayed on track and invested in what he knew

If I was to be confined to one end of the playing field, then I was going to be a star on that part of the playing field.

—Colin Powell

best. When the tech bubble burst in 2000, he was largely protected from the drastic losses other investors incurred.

Through hard experience, we have learned the value of sticking to what we know. We have learned to avoid the hot tips offered by colleagues at the water cooler, the latest trends touted in the media, and the unwelcome plugs from stockbrokers. *Sticking to what you know* helps reduce your chances of placing bets on high-risk investments.

Maybe this deserves a little more explanation. We have consistently followed a long-term approach to wealth building, and this book takes that same approach. Placing big bets on high-risk investments creates way too much downside exposure. And while you may recover from a wipeout, the chances are against you.

Perhaps the exception to this rule is early in your career, when you have little to lose. The problem with this exception is that should you be right on your risky play, you may be tempted to make these kinds of bets all the time—and eventually, you'll get wiped out.

We all get caught up in our successes. This kind of luck can easily turn into arrogance. To continue investing successfully for the long term, you must stay vigilant and humble. You must not let yourself be carried away, even by your own success.

Investment Strategy No. 9: Pay Fair Value for the Right Advice

We are in the business of helping people learn how to make money. We want everyone to learn how to make money, so that they don't have to rely on someone else. Unfortunately, some people think they should do everything themselves and never hire anyone to help them. In almost every case, that's a mistake. If a good professional can make you more money than you pay him or her, why not use that professional?

The real key to determining the worth of a broker or other financial professional is to monitor her or his results and make sure that you are getting what you are paying for. Pick your financial professionals *at least as carefully* as you select your car. (See Chapter 9.) Ask friends and colleagues whom they use, who is successful, and why. Interview several professionals

It's always been my philosophy to hire the best and get out of the way.

—Donald Rumsfeld

to find someone whom you can relate to. If you can't communicate with someone, that person will be of little help to you.

Investment Strategy No. 10: Invest Some of Your Money Internationally

The world is becoming a smaller place from a financial standpoint. But while the world's economies are increasingly tied together, there are still many financial markets that offer different opportunities from the U.S. market. Investing in these markets diversifies your portfolio, allowing you to take advantage of different economies and markets.

China and other Pacific Rim countries, for example, are experiencing very rapid growth, and that growth is likely to continue for years to come. China, in particular, has enormous potential, as the most populous nation in the world is introduced to private ownership and unprecedented entrepreneurial opportunities. By investing in these countries (or specific companies based there), you add another layer of diversity to your portfolio.

The easiest way to invest overseas is through international mutual funds or the aforementioned exchange-traded funds. Individual foreign stocks are more difficult to manage, because you have to consider currency fluctuations in addition to the economic circumstances of another country. All things considered, you should probably leave these kinds of problems to professional managers. But buying "baskets" of stocks in the form of a low-cost interna-

In the emerging global economy, everything is mobile: capital, factories, even entire industries.

—William Jefferson Clinton

tional fund or ETF will provide access to these markets, while helping you to avoid the headaches that might arise from buying individual companies' stocks.

If you are determined to invest in individual companies in non-U.S. markets, there is a convenient way to accomplish this: by buying American Depository Receipts (ADRs). An ADR is a stock equivalent instrument of an overseas company that trades on a U.S. exchange just like any other U.S. stock.

Investment Strategy No. 11: Use Barometers, Indicators, and Trends to Improve Your Investing

It may seem overwhelming to have to make sense of all the investing choices that are available to you. With practice, however, you'll get the hang of it. Soon enough, you'll be able to create your own playbook. Meanwhile, another good tactic is to use market indicators to help you gauge whether stocks might be moving up or down. We look at a few of our own favorites here.

Watch Key Barometers of the Stock Market

Economics isn't everyone's cup of tea, to say the least. But learning to watch a few key indicators can make investing much easier for you. Inflation and long-term interest rates are two of the most telling indicators, and the signs they reveal are fairly easy to interpret.

If they are both rising, the stock market has a strong likelihood of falling, and you might opt to shift to other investments. Conversely, if both inflation and long-term rates are falling, the stock market has a very good chance of moving upward.

These are good general rules that can help even novice investors make general forecasts without engaging in wild predictions. Both indicators are very important and should be followed closely. Once you get a feel for these connections, you should be able to watch the nightly news and, based on what you hear, have some basic understanding about where the economy and the stock market may be headed.

Interest rates and inflation also have thresholds that are commonly referred to as *pivot points*. Moves above a pivot point have a greater impact on the market than moves below the pivot point. For long-term interest rates, the pivot point has generally been 10 percent, and for inflation, 3 to 4 percent. So, for example, if long-term interest rates move above 10 percent and inflation moves above 4 percent, the chance of having a weak stock market is greater.

Use Housing Starts as an Economic Indicator

Increases in housing starts (the number of new houses being built) can be used as a key indicator for investing in companies that are involved in construction or the production of household goods. But more generally, strong housing starts is a good indicator of a growing economy, because it means that a number of players are willing to take the risks necessary to build, buy, and finance the houses. When all these different players (the builders, buyers, and mortgage companies) are moving in one direction, it is a positive indicator.

Keep in mind that this phenomenon also works in reverse. When housing starts fall off, this is a reliable indicator of a slowing economy. It may be time for a pullback not only from real estate–related stocks, but also from the stock market more generally.

TIME-SAVING, WEALTH-BUILDING TIPS

Yes, there are a lot of things to keep track of as you embark on your path to financial freedom. Soon enough, though, you'll discover some shortcuts that will help ease the way. In the meantime, we offer some ideas to help you build up your confidence.

Investment Strategy No. 12: Use Internet Investing for the Lowest Transaction Costs

Part of your investment strategy should be to minimize transaction costs, that is, the cost of buying and selling the things you invest in. The Internet has emerged as one of the fastest and cheapest ways to move your money from one investment to another. Traditional brokerage firms now offer high-speed, direct-access trading that gives you the best price on your stocks at the lowest transaction cost, mainly because it can be done on the computer without human intervention on their part.

Of course, this means a lower level of service. You need to make sure that you are getting what you need *at the best trade cost for you.* Sometimes customer service is worth paying a little more for; sometimes it isn't.

A word of caution: The explosive growth of the Internet has attracted not just reputable people and companies, but also kooks and con artists. If you use the Internet to do financial transactions (and we argue that you should, unless you need special kinds of services), you are almost certain to be exposed to fraudulent schemes and illegal stock promotions. Don't bite.

Use the Internet to help you with your *research*. Then, after you've made your decisions about particular investments, use the Internet to *buy* and *sell*. Don't use the Internet as a supermarket or a bazaar. You're very likely to get burned if you do.

Investment Strategy No. 13: Don't Make Investments Purely for Tax Reasons

Never make an investment solely for tax reasons. All too frequently, investors have been sold poor investments that promised high tax savings. Blinded by the possibility of avoiding a guaranteed tax payment, investors have ignored risks that they wouldn't normally have taken. What do they wind up with? Well, a bad investment. In addition, they often wind up with an audit and a disallowance of the tax savings—a true double whammy. Yes, there are exceptions to this rule. For the most part, though, people who make investments simply for the associated tax shelter wind up being unhappy with that decision.

If a good investment also has tax advantages, *great*. But let that be an extra benefit, rather than the main benefit.

Investment Strategy No. 14: Keep a Journal of Your Best and Worst Ideas

We have kept a log of investment lessons we have learned over the years. We still use it today as we make our investments. (We've also used it in writing this book.) Of course, we'd like to believe that we remember every lesson that we've ever learned as the result of our past successes and mistakes (especially the mistakes!), but the truth is, we don't. A good set of notes, lined up chronologically, can be an invaluable tool.

Try it. Get a diary or journal book, or simply a bound book with blank lined pages, and start making notes in it. If you get ideas based on what you read in *this* book, jot them down in your own book. As you make investment decisions, record those decisions. Pat yourself on the back (in writing) when you do something smart. When you decide that you wish you had done something differently, note that, too. Over the years, your investment journal will become a valuable tool.

YOUR MISSION TO WEALTH TO-DO LIST

1. GET OUT OF DEBT. We'll say this as often as we can. Until you've paid off your credit cards, with their staggering interest rates of 16 percent or higher, you don't have to go out in search of a great wealth builder. It's sitting right in front of you. Pay off those cards, and don't ever let yourself fall down that same well again.

2. START SMALL AND SCALE UP. You don't have to get everything right all at once. Learn a particular investment technique. Get good at it. Then learn another one, and get good at that one. Expand your repertoire slowly. The good news is that you can use the same techniques to manage a lot of money that you use to manage a small amount of money. So *get good at the fundamentals* early; they'll serve you forever.

3. **DIVERSIFY AND PERSONALIZE.** Diversifying your investments makes sense for several reasons. First, it protects you from overexposure to a single sector or product line. Second, it introduces you to a broader range of vehicles and strategies. Gradually, you'll find the mix of instruments that's right for you. Remember, there is no "one best investment" or "one best strategy." The best investment is the one that's best *for you.*

4. **PAY FOR (ONLY) THE HELP YOU NEED.** We've made this suggestion in previous chapters: Figure out where you need help, and pay a fair price for that help. One specific example is buying and selling stocks: If you want hands-on help, be prepared to pay extra for a broker's services. (And keep track of how good those services are!)

5. **DEVELOP YOUR INSTINCTS.** Keep your eye on a few key indicators, such as housing starts. Watch the nightly news, or read the *Wall Street Journal.* Look for the bigger patterns and trends. Gradually, your investing instincts will get better and better.

6. **KEEP A JOURNAL.** If you (or we) had a perfect memory, this advice wouldn't be necessary. You need a record of what you've done right and what you've done wrong, and *why.* Keeping a journal, arranged chronologically, is the best way of guaranteeing that you'll have access to everything you've learned about investing as you progress down the road to financial freedom.

★ ★ ★

CHAPTER 11

Implementing Your Investment Plan

Use steamroller strategy; that is, make up your mind on course and direction of action, and stick to it.

—George S. Patton

Once you've gotten a grasp of the investing strategies that suit you best, it's time to put them into action. There are many ways to accomplish that as you move your money from one investment to another. In this chapter, we'll look at how to make the most of money market accounts, margin, and placing orders.

MANAGING YOUR INVESTMENT ACCOUNTS

Sometimes, taking the first step is the most difficult. You may already have an idea of some of the companies in which you'd like to invest. You may not be exactly sure how to get started, though. Before you start writing checks and waiting for stock certificates to arrive in the mail, you first need to get your accounts in order.

Investment Plan Strategy No. 1: Open a Brokerage Money Market Account

One of your first investment moves should be to open a brokerage money market account as your investment holding account. In other words, the money market account serves as a sort of "home base" for your money.

Whenever you save a little extra money, you should immediately put that money into your money market account, where it will wait until you figure out its investment destination. No, you won't get rich by putting assets into a money market account, but it is a safe haven to work from.

You have three basic choices, in terms of where to locate your money market account: a bank, a mutual fund family like Fidelity or Vanguard, or a brokerage firm (either full-service or discount). As a rule, banks are our least favorite choice. They generally pay a lower rate of interest than a brokerage firm. Also, unless the bank you select has a securities firm as part of its holding company, it will be more cumbersome to use your money market account as a home base as you move your money into other investments.

The second option is to open your account with a major mutual fund family such as Fidelity or Vanguard. This makes the most sense if you plan on doing a lot of mutual fund investing. You would start working with (for example) Vanguard by opening a mutual fund money market account, then moving your money from that account to others when you decide which funds make the most sense for you.

The important points to consider when picking a mutual fund family are *price, range of fund options,* and *service.* Fidelity and Vanguard are both known for their good service. Fidelity has one of the largest selections of funds, particularly in the sector end of the business. (This simply means a fund that focuses on a specific sector, like technology or health care.) Vanguard, on the other hand, is known for its lower fee structure—meaning lower costs to you.

If you use a brokerage firm, you have two choices: a full-service firm or a discount broker. As a rule, we recommend a discount broker, for two reasons. The first is *price.* When you're dealing with a discount broker, you can buy or sell up to 1,000 shares of a stock for as little as $10 in commissions. The full-service firm has to charge much higher commissions to cover the costs of the services that it provides to you.

The second reason to go with a discount brokerage is that you are less likely to be pressured to buy a product developed by the company itself. If you use a full-service brokerage firm, it will eventually assign your account to a broker, who will call you with the latest "great" investment idea. While this isn't necessarily bad, we would prefer to have you free of this kind of pressure while you're learning the fundamentals of investing. Later on, you may find that an experienced broker who knows what he or she is doing and has some specialized knowledge will serve you well. When you *do* find such a financial professional, don't be afraid to pay for the service. The broker has to make money for his or her skill and good advice—and a broker who is good will earn the fee many times over.

Meanwhile, consider a discount broker such as Charles Schwab (1-800-544-9797) or T.D. Waterhouse (1-800-233-3417). Or, if you're so inclined, feel free to contact our own family firm, PremiereTrade Securities (1-800-620-8723) and ask about our services.

As always, remember that you're shopping. When you shop around for a money market account, compare yields (what the account pays you), the services the account might offer you, and the charges for those services. Understand what the fees buy you, and be sure to balance price issues against important considerations like customer support. If you want more help, be prepared to pay a little more.

Investment Plan Strategy No. 2: Understand the Benefits and Risks of Buying on Margin

Many investors have found margin accounts to be useful tools in expanding their investment holdings.

Margin arrangements in the stock market allow you to borrow up to 50 percent of the value of your account to buy more investments. A margin account is one in which stocks can be purchased for a combination of cash and a loan. The collateral is actually the stock itself. Margin accounts for other investments, such as FOREX and commodities, allow you to borrow even more.

Margin isn't good or bad in and of itself. Margin is simply *leverage*. If your trade is favorable, you will be helped by margin. Conversely, if your trade is bad, the added leverage will increase your loss.

Buying stocks on margin makes profitable investing more challenging, because your investments must earn more than the interest rate (margin rate) you are paying on the money you have borrowed. The lower the interest rate on your margin account, the better your chances of making money on the money you borrow. For example, if your margin interest rate is 8 percent and you are earning only 6 percent on your investment, you are losing 2 percent just for the privilege of borrowing the money to invest.

Buying on margin can be *risky*. In a down, or bear, market, you lose the equity in the stock you own, plus the equity in the additional stock you bought on margin (unless you are shorting, or selling stock that you have borrowed in the hope of buying it back later at a lower price). In addition, you must also pay interest on the money you borrowed to buy more stock. Absent some great market reversal, eventually you must repay the loan, with interest, and take your losses.

We assure you that all this makes for a *very bad day*, indeed. We know, because we have had some days just like that. Margin loans can be a way to boost your yield, but they can

> *Good will, like a good name, is got by many actions and lost by one.*
> —Lord Jeffrey

also wipe you out. All in all, you are best advised to wait until you are very comfortable with your investment strategy and emotionally ready to handle an unexpected loss before you trade on margin.

Investment Plan Strategy No. 3: Don't Invest All Your Money in One Day

Once you're ready to invest, it may be tempting to get all your cash working at once. Resist the temptation. As a rule, you shouldn't invest all of your money in the stock market on the same day. That's the kind of move that exposes you to potential blips in the market that may hit the day after you buy. There are few investment experiences worse than watching something you just bought hit the skids right after you buy it.

On the other hand, don't spread the investment out over too many months. That strategy may cost you a great deal in terms of profits if the market rises very quickly. Since most big gains in the stock market occur in one or two spurts during the year, an investment delay could cost your account most of the potential profit for the year.

The best compromise is to divide your investment into thirds and invest those thirds over several weeks. If the market takes a downturn during this period, relax and wait for the market to correct itself and move forward again before investing the balance of your funds. This strategy is called *incremental investing*, and it is an excellent technique for easing your way into the market.

Some investors use a similar method to exit from a particular investment. If an investment reaches your target goal, sell 75 percent of it and take your profits. Keep 25 percent in the market for higher gains.

If you are going to achieve excellence in big things, you develop the habit in little matters.

—Colin Powell

Incremental investing (and disinvesting) has some of the same attributes as the technique called *dollar cost averaging.* The difference between the two is that the dollar cost averaging method promotes investing on a regular, consistent basis, regardless of the direction of the market or the investment you are targeting. Incremental investing dictates that you invest your money *only* when the investment is moving in a favorable direction.

MUTUAL FUNDS FOR DIVERSITY AND SIMPLICITY

Knowing how to invest and *where* to invest go hand in hand. One of the easiest places to start is in mutual funds, which can provide instant diversification. But with literally thousands of mutual funds available to investors today, choosing a mutual fund can be extremely challenging. Next, we'll look at some tips for including mutual funds in your investment arsenal.

Investment Plan Strategy No. 4: Use No-Load or Low-Load Mutual Funds to Reduce Your Costs

Mutual funds are popular investments because they are easy to understand, have built-in management, and perform well for most people. By and large, they are marketed in different "wrappers" in order to attract different buyers.

There are four different types of funds based on their cost structure:

1. *Class A shares.* These funds charge a front-end "load" (or commission) when you invest.
2. *Class B shares.* These funds do not charge a load when you invest, but they have a "reverse load" when you sell. This is commonly called a surrender charge, and in most cases the fee declines the longer you stay in the fund. The amount is usually 5 percent to 6 percent the first year, and this number goes down by 1 percent each year.
3. *Class C or "level load" funds.* These funds charge a higher annual expense charge, which levels out what you would have paid in the case of the A or B shares.
4. *"No-load" funds.* These funds charge no additional fees for marketing costs. Sometimes their operating expenses are a little higher, but a little comparison shopping will give you a better picture of each fund. Contrary to some people's opinion, there is no real evidence that load funds outperform no-load funds.

The bottom line for you as an investor is that you need to do a good bit of homework before you make a final decision on whether a certain fund is best for you. When investigating a fund, determine what its return has been *net of all loads, fees, and cost.* The total return number you calculate will tell you whether any added expenses are worth it.

Discipline is the soul of an army.

—George Washington

How can you find out how a particular fund is doing? One of the best sources is Morningstar.com. Morningstar rates most of the thousands of funds and gives in-depth information on a number of areas:

* The fund's one-year, three-year, five-year, and ten-year performance
* All fees and expense ratios associated with the fund
* A star rating, from one to five (five is best)
* The fund's manager, and how long he or she has run the fund

There are now something like 8,000 mutual funds from which you can choose. Here are four factors to consider when trying to decide among them:

* *Look at the three-year to five-year track record for long-term performance.* You want to make sure that the fund has had some reasonable success over the long term. Going out five years gives you more comfort about the stability of the fund, but we think shorter time periods give you a stronger indication of how the fund is doing now, under the present market scenario and current management. Clearly, both views are important.

  Picking new funds is a specialty you'll want to save until later. Meanwhile, track records are extremely important. The regulators stress (and compel all funds to remind you) that past performance is no guarantee of future success. While that's true, we also think that past performance does give you great insight into how the management has performed in a certain economic period. This is particularly true in comparison to other similar funds. It isn't a guarantee, but it is good information.

★ *Make sure the same management is in place.* If it isn't, the track record isn't particularly relevant. Managers change more than the funds want you to believe. With so much money on the line, hot managers get offers, just like big-time athletes. If you find a good manager, stick with him or her. If that manager goes elsewhere, you may want to transfer some funds in that direction if the new fund also meets your objectives.

★ *Confirm that the fund's one-month and three-month performance are still positive.* While the three-year performance is important, you obviously don't want to invest in a fund just as it's on its way down. Before you buy, get an update on its current performance numbers. Make sure the fund is still doing what you want. If the current trend is in a pullback or retracement, wait until it resumes its upward journey before you put your money into it.

★ *Make sure the fund fits your overall investment philosophy.* If you're very conservative, you shouldn't have a lot of your money in aggressive growth funds. The funds are labeled by objectives, so make sure the fund you pick fits your particular profile. One caution, here: The objectives listed are usually very broad. Look beyond the wording, and ask the managers the type of securities the fund is actually holding. If the fund is called a growth fund, but it has a lot of cash and bonds in its portfolio, the fund may be too conservative for your needs. The bottom line is to exercise care and match your funds' investment objectives to your own.

Investment Plan Strategy No. 5: Don't Buy the "Fund of the Month"

All the big business and financial magazines, newspapers, and newsletters tout the "hot new fund of the month." While you may want to jot down the name for future research, stop there.

There are many reasons for a fund to spike to the top in a given month. You shouldn't be interested in that. You want consistent winners that are still performing. Look for the turtle, not the hare.

FUNDAMENTALS OF BUYING STOCK

When most people think of investing, they think of buying stock. With tens of thousands of companies in the United States and abroad, though, choosing the stocks that are right for your portfolio can be a real challenge.

Investment Plan Strategy No. 6: Look for Healthy Companies That Are Also Competitive Leaders

One approach that top analysts use to select new stock buys is to look for leaders. But even if a company has been a long-term leader, if it's losing market share to its competition, it may be headed for a fall. Watch for these key points:

★ The company you select should have a leading product in the industry.

★ The company should have widely recognized brands.

★ Look for consistent revenue and earnings growth.

★ Look for excellent profit margins.

This type of stock analysis combines a fundamental analysis of the *industry* and the *individual company*. Most great investors put prospective investments through a screen like this.

Investment Plan Strategy No. 7: Buy the Best Stock in the Best Industry in a Strong Market

This sounds easy, so why don't more people do it? For the most part, the answer is *lack of patience*. As we have just discussed, it is wise to invest in the general direction of the market. It is also true that you are generally better off investing in the leading industry or sector. Finally, if those two rules work, find the strongest stock in the leading industry, and you should have a winner.

There are many stock-screening software programs and Web sites that will give you this type of information. YahooFinance.com is one such site. Using information of this type, you can determine

1. Whether the market is trending up
2. What sectors or areas are leading the market
3. What stocks in those sectors are performing the best

Following this thought process, you would buy a stock if it met these criteria as long as you thought the trend of the market would continue upward.

Investment Plan Strategy No. 8: Don't Buy a Low-Priced Stock Because You Think It's Cheap

New investors frequently get hurt buying low-priced stocks, which they do mainly because they can buy a lot of shares. But in many cases, these stocks are heavily touted by telephone solicitors, who pump the stock up to unrealistic levels. As a result, the people who invest in these stocks are unlikely to win.

Don't iron when the strike is hot.

—Anonymous

In fact, there is no direct correlation between low price and great buys. Only the fundamentals underlying the stock, current market conditions, and technical indicators of the stock should be used to decide whether to buy or sell. There must be more than just a cheap price, or you're likely to get just a cheap stock with little upside.

Investment Plan Strategy No. 9: Place the Right Type of Order at the Right Time

There are several types of orders that you can place with your broker, and the type you choose can affect your return:

★ *Market order.* A market order is simply an order to have stock bought or sold immediately, as soon as your order hits the market. The positive is that your order will be executed quickly. The negative is that in a fast-moving market, the price may get away from you.

★ *Limit order.* A limit order allows you to set your price. It is an instruction to your broker that if you can't get exactly that price or better, you don't want the trade. Many traders won't trade without using a limit order. Others feel that the exact price they get isn't as important as getting in on the trend. We agree with the latter.

★ *Stop loss order.* One of the most important order instructions is the protective sell order that you place to protect your downside. The stop loss order indicates that should your position trade at this price, you want to sell. At that point, the stop loss order changes into a market order, and your position is sold as quickly as possible, even though, in a fast-moving market, you may not get the exact price you wanted.

★ *Day order.* This is an instruction to the broker that is good for just one day; if the order is not filled that day, it is cancelled.

★ *Good till canceled.* This is an important instruction to use, because, as the name implies your order is preserved until you cancel it. It is frequently used with a stop loss order to guarantee some gains, or with a limit order to sell the stock when it reaches your price goal.

Investment Plan Strategy No. 10: Investigate IPOs for New Profit Opportunities

An initial public offering (IPO) is the first offering of a company's securities to the public. While a great deal of work and planning goes into setting the initial price, it is frequently set on the low end of the expected range in order to make sure that the entire offering sells out, and to create excitement about the company and new buyers as the price rises. Unfortunately, the price can run up fast, resulting in an equally exciting (but unpleasant) pullback in price. Where there is volatility in price, there is opportunity for gain on either the short side, the long side, or both.

As a rule, IPOs are not an investment vehicle for the faint of heart. On the other hand, they can be very profitable for the trader who learns to follow them.

INVEST IN BONDS

Many investors stop at mutual funds and stocks, believing that's all they need to round out their investments. But, as we mentioned previously, it takes more than stocks to reduce the risk in a diversified investment portfolio.

Bonds can play a very important role in diversity, because they give you a fixed rate of return with a lower risk classification than stocks. This does not mean that all bonds are without risk. In fact, bonds are classified from very high-grade investments to low-grade, with the latter group sometimes being referred to as "junk bonds." Even within a particular grade, you can increase or decrease your risk depending on whether you use leverage, whether you buy individual bonds instead of a bond mutual fund, or what the time to maturity of your bond portfolio is.

Investment Plan Strategy No. 11: Shop the Yield You Are Offered on Your Fixed-Rate Investments

Earlier in this book, we suggested looking for the lowest-interest-rate credit cards. When investing, do the opposite: Try to get the highest yield, or interest rate, on your money.

Simply shopping around as you would for any other product can get you higher returns. Doing research for this book, for example, we checked several local banks and found a 1/2 percent difference among their money market savings accounts and more than a 1 percent per year difference between the banks' money market accounts and what a mutual fund or brokerage money market account would pay you. Check around; it's worth the effort.

Not all yields are the same. If you ask a broker what the yield is on a bond you are considering, you have to be specific about the *type* of yield you are seeking, or you are likely to be quoted the most favorable yield. It is crucial that you understand the types of yields—otherwise you'll get taken to the proverbial cleaners.

For example, a $10,000 bond at 6 percent interest has a *coupon rate* of 6 percent and a *nominal rate* of the same 6 percent. However, if the bond is currently selling at a premium because interest rates had fallen, your *yield to maturity* will be lower than 6 percent, because when the bond matures, you will receive only $10,000 even though you paid more.

Even worse, if the bond has a call provision and this provision is exercised because rates changed, your *yield to call* will be even lower. While these arithmetic examples may seem like sleight of hand, they really are nothing more than an illustration of making sure you ask the right questions.

If you buy bonds when their yields hit historic highs, you have a good opportunity to profit on both the high yield and the capital gains that will result when interest rates fall and the value of the bond rises. When interest rates fall, newly issued bonds will pay less, and the value of your higher-interest bonds will increase. When this occurs, you can sell your bonds for a capital gain, boosting your overall return.

For more aggressive investors, consider buying zero-coupon bonds, which offer leverage and give you the opportunity for even higher yields. Zero-coupon bonds do not pay current interest and therefore cost less, but gain in value as interest rates fall.

Another way to profit from this interest-rate move is to buy mutual funds with specific target maturities. Century Target Maturities is one investment company that offers a wide range of portfolios with different maturities. Remember that it is in a rapidly declining interest-rate environment that bonds have the best chance to outperform stocks.

In a rising-interest-rate environment, long-term bonds will lose value (equity) as rates rise. Unless you hold the bond to its actual redemption date, you will lose more value in the bond with each rise in market rates. This is because a buyer will pay less for your bond, which carries a lower rate, than for a newly issued bond paying a higher rate. Although the amount of your loss differs depending on the interest-rate spread, a rule of thumb on a 30-year bond is that it will lose 10 percent of its value for every 1 percent rise in interest rates.

Investment Plan Strategy No. 12: Consider Junk Bonds for High Yield

Junk bonds got their name because of the low value associated with those bonds, which were thought to have a high default risk because the issuer wasn't considered a good credit risk. Nevertheless, higher risk generally means a higher potential return, and in the bond world, that means a higher interest rate.

You can mitigate some of the risk involved by buying a mix of junk bonds, using a bond mutual fund as your investment vehicle. This will increase the diversity of the bonds within the mutual fund holding. You could diversify by buying a junk bond mutual fund that would provide the mix of bonds for you.

Investment Plan Strategy No. 13: Ladder Your Bonds

"Laddering" is a useful tool for investors, helping to time the maturities of the bonds in your portfolio. The point is to make sure that some of your bonds mature each year, so that you don't have to sell prior to maturity and take a capital loss.

A portfolio of bonds with varying maturity dates is considered a laddered portfolio. Laddering bonds gives you extra protection and flexibility. If one of your bonds appreciates because interest rates fall, you can sell it and take the capital gain. If interest rates rise, you aren't trapped in all long-term bonds with the same maturity— that is, bonds that have gone down in value as interest rates rose.

Some of your bonds will come due on earlier maturity dates, and if interest rates have risen, you can reinvest that money in new bonds at higher rates. You will hold the older bonds until their maturity dates. This means that you will be receiving lower returns on your current bonds than on the new issues, but you aren't forced to sell early and take a capital loss because rates have fallen.

A laddered bond portfolio created over a period of years allows an investor to live on a steady stream of income. As bonds come due, the proceeds are reinvested in the new interest-rate environment, with a plan to hold the new bonds to a predetermined date.

SPECIALIZED MARKETS FOR DIVERSITY

Many people believe that, if they have mutual funds, stocks, and bonds in their portfolio, they're all set—that these three types of investments will cover all their needs. That may be, but there is a world of investing opportunities beyond that. From options to FOREX, investors should keep the doors open to alternatives that may be suitable for their investing styles. These are more sophisticated and complex investments, so we highly recommend that you move slowly and become well educated before diving into these investments.

Investment Plan Strategy No. 14: Add Options to Your Portfolio

Stock options are simply the right to buy or sell the underlying security (the security behind the option) at a predetermined price sometime in the future. When the market is doing well, options are promoted as a way to make more money with less capital.

For example, you may buy an option to buy 100 shares of IBM at a price of 75 three months out. This means that during the term of that option, you have the right to buy 100 shares of IBM at the *strike price* of 75. If the stock never reaches 75 during that term, your option becomes worthless. That's because any investor can buy IBM at a price below 75. If, however, IBM reaches, say, 80, before the strike date, then each of the 100 shares covered by that option is now worth $5.00, giving you a profit of $500. (This may be a tough concept to digest all at once, but be patient and read on.)

While it is true you can make a lot of money with options, option leverage is not the same as leverage in investments such as real estate. The reason is that the stock market is considerably more volatile than the real estate market, and stock options are frequently shorter in terms of time periods and can be a rapidly wasting asset.

Please heed our caution: Because of the market's volatility, option investors can lose all of their investment very quickly if the market turns against them. This is true even in a market that is generally considered a bull market because your time value of holding the option is reducing each day, thus reducing your options value. Also, whenever you use high leverage, you must remember that losses can mount very quickly. We aren't saying *not* to use leverage, because we use it ourselves; what we are saying is that all investors must understand the risks and be able to accept them, both mentally and financially. We do not recommend plunging into the options market until you are a more seasoned investor.

However, options are interesting investment vehicles because they can be used conservatively to offset other holdings you may have, or as a hedge against a block of stock.

The purpose is clear. It is safety with solvency.
—Dwight D. Eisenhower

Like many investments, options require education, so that you can understand how to analyze your risk versus your potential rewards. For more information, try the Chicago Board of Options Exchange (www.cboe.com); it has a great deal of free educational information that you can start your training with.

Investment Plan Strategy No. 15: Use Commodities as a Hedge

Commodity trading is a high-leverage investment in commodity goods such as corn, lumber, oil, or pork bellies. The original purpose of this market was to provide commodity producers and users a way to protect themselves against price changes on these products in the future. Many people today, however, use the commodity markets as an alternative investment to the stock market, since commodities tend to run counter to the stock market and can act as a hedge.

Investing directly in commodities requires specialized education, because it has high leverage and correspondingly higher risk than the stock market. Recently, however, new mutual funds have opened up that are designed to mimic the commodities index or the performance of a particular commodity, like gold.

Commodity-based mutual funds are relatively new, and should be considered more aggressive than a broad market index. But for a small part of your portfolio, they may offer you another diversification tool, particularly since they can run counter to the stock market. Two fund offerings are PIMCO Commodity Real Return Strategy Fund (PCRAX) and Oppenheimer Real Asset Fund (QRAAX).

SPECIAL STOCK MARKET CONDITIONS
YOU CAN SPECIALIZE IN TO CREATE ADDED VALUE

The following five special market situations offer unique possibilities for you to create added value:

1. *Spin-offs.* Companies frequently spin off product lines into separate companies. These new companies have proved to be profitable investments because they can specialize in their core business and not be held back by unrelated and underperforming businesses. The company that spins off the other one will also make a lot on the spin-off, so consider that company as well. Watch the movement of the stock price carefully when the announcement is first made. Generally, the stock will continue to move in that direction until the spin-off is complete, then the stock frequently pulls back.

2. *Splits.* When the stock price of a company rises to higher dollar amounts, the directors will frequently split the shares 2 for 1 (or by some other fractions) in order to bring the price per share down. A lower cost per share

helps small investors stay active in the company's stock, because of the psychological factor that they can have more shares for the same price. The best time to take advantage of this situation is from the announcement of the split up to the time of the actual split. After the split actually occurs, the stock tends to settle in for some time, until investors believe the underlying value is strong enough to push it forward.

3. *Buybacks.* Watch for companies that have active buyback programs. Buybacks occur when the company believes it can create stronger value for its shareholders by using corporate cash to purchase its own stock in the open market instead of investing in something else. As stock is purchased by the company and taken out of circulation, the remaining stock tends to increase in value faster. While stock buybacks are sometimes used just to bolster a lagging stock, they are normally considered a very positive sign.

4. *Low debt.* Just as high debt inhibits personal financial growth, high debt loads (and the associated high interest payments) hurt corporate profits. Lower profits ultimately result in lower share price. Watch companies carefully as interest rates change. If they have a lot of debt and rates go up, they will have to spend more of their profit to pay interest.

5. *Insider buying.* There are many reasons for corporate insiders to sell stock that they have. Some are personal reasons, and that isn't important in considering whether you want to buy the stock or not. But there is usually only one reason that corporate insiders buy their corporation's

stock, and that's because they think it will go up in value. They may not always be right, but since they know the company best, it is a strong indication. Use this information as a positive sign to investigate further. It isn't a guarantee, since sometimes insiders buy as a sign of good faith. Nevertheless, it is an important indicator.

Investment Plan Strategy No. 16: Buy Precious Metals as a Hedge against Inflation

It is possible to make money investing in precious metals, but very few people ever do. We have told our clients for many years that they are much better off buying gold to wear than as an investment. So far, we've been right. One day that may change, but the evidence of history to date has been overwhelming.

I know no way of judging the future but by the past.
—Patrick Henry

Nevertheless, gold (traditionally the leading precious metal) has historically been an excellent hedge against inflation. When our country's inflation begins to rise, gold could serve a useful diversifying role in your portfolio.

If you *do* decide to invest in precious metals, remember that they are a more aggressive investment than stocks. Consequently, investments of this type should be limited to that portion of your portfolio that is allocated to speculation.

Any time you enter a more speculative area, you should consider using a mutual fund that offers professional management or an ETF (exchange-traded fund). If you have an interest in this area of investing, the ETF helps you avoid buying and storing gold yourself, and frees you of the disposition headache and cost.

Investment Plan Strategy No. 17: Buy Real Estate Investment Trusts (REITs) for Income and Appreciation

American investors have a love-hate relationship with REITs, because historically they have offered high income, but there was frequently a capital loss on their sale. The reason for this was not so much the investor's fault as the result of insufficient information provided by the salesperson.

REITs have traditionally been sold as a long-term buy and hold vehicle. The problem here is that REITs fluctuate in value, just like the underlying real estate they hold. You cannot simply buy and hold without regard to an exit date, or you may be selling during a decline in the market.

REITs come in two basic types: equity and mortgage. If you own an equity REIT, you own part of the property in the REIT. You have the opportunity to profit both from the rental income and from the capital gains from property appreciation. In a mortgage REIT, you take on the role of lender. You make a more predictable income from the interest the REIT receives, and there is usually some opportunity for capital gain from the mortgages' equity participation in the property.

Just like owning real estate yourself, participating in a REIT affords good opportunities in strong real estate markets and higher risks in weak ones.

Investment Plan Strategy No. 18: Investigate FOREX, the World's Largest Financial Marketplace

FOREX (Foreign Currency Exchange) is the world's largest financial marketplace. In recent years, FOREX has been opened to individual investors. Trading in foreign currency has always been well known in other parts of the world, because using other countries' currencies has been commonplace. U.S. investors are now beginning to involve themselves in this market.

As with all investments, there are advantages and disadvantages. The biggest advantage is that there are only six major currency pairs that a trader has to follow, as opposed to tens of thousands of stocks. While there are buy and sell spreads, there are no commissions, and trading is available at more flexible hours for people who have a day job.

Both an advantage and disadvantage of the FOREX market is the leverage of 100 to 1, compared with (for example) the typical 2-to-1 ratio in the stock market. As we have said with other investments, when you work on high leverage, you have a corresponding higher risk, and you absolutely *have* to understand that risk before you start investing. The flip side or advantage of leverage is that you need only a small amount of cash to control a large position.

YOUR MISSION TO WEALTH TO-DO LIST

1. SET UP A MONEY MARKET ACCOUNT FIRST. There are a lot of places to house such an account, but you can't really get started in investing until you have a home base for your money. Look for the right combination of yield, service, and cost.

2. LEARN THE FUNDAMENTALS OF MARGIN INVESTING AND PHASED INVESTING. Leverage is a key principle in investing. You have to understand how it can work

either for you or against you. (Don't *ever* trade on margin without a complete understanding of your exposure in the worst case.) Go in and out of the market quickly, but not precipitously. Learn and apply the one-third/one-third/one-third approach.

3. LEARN HOW TO USE MUTUAL FUNDS. For ease of investment, nothing beats mutual funds. And if you're working with nontaxable accounts like IRAs, you don't even have to worry about the tax implications of your trades. (That comes later in life.) Carefully consider the different classes of mutual funds, and how (and how much) you want to pay.

4. STUDY THE FUNDAMENTALS OF STOCK INVESTING. Don't buy cheap; buy *good*. Most great investors look for a combination of the right company in the right industry. Buy and sell using the right instructions to your broker. Keep your eye out for IPO opportunities— these are often hard to get in on, but they can be worth the effort.

5. USE BONDS TO DIVERSIFY YOUR PORTFOLIO. Bonds often move in the opposite direction from the stock market, and therefore they can help you mitigate the risks inherent in trading stocks. Before investing in bonds, get a feel for the *range* of bonds that are out there, and which fit most comfortably into your strategy. Remember that some bonds are risky (and tend to have correspondingly high returns).

6. EXPLORE THE SPECIALIZED MARKETS. Commodities, options, precious metals, REITs, and foreign currency may have a place in your portfolio. Each has its own risks and rewards; consider them carefully before taking the plunge.

★ ★ ★

CHAPTER 12

Maximizing Your Retirement Plan

Wealth is not his that has it, but his that enjoys it.

—Benjamin Franklin

I f you're like many American workers, your most important long-term asset is likely to be your retirement plan. While there was a time when a worker had little or no input into the investment of his or her retirement money, today that has changed. The corporate disasters of large companies such as Enron and WorldCom wiped out employee retirement plans and focused an intense spotlight on the potential hazards of corporate retirement plans.

Today, if you practice the see-no-evil, hear-no-evil philosophy toward your retirement nest egg, you may wind up wondering what happened to all the eggs. Not only should you be concerned about how your retirement money is invested, but you should also make sure that your retirement plan is being properly funded—and that the company you work for keeps its hand out of the pension cookie jar. This is not only important; it is a necessity.

Those that believe money can do everything are frequently prepared to do everything for money.

—Anonymous

Companies can and do borrow from employees' pension plans or restructure them in order for certain employees to benefit more than others from them. While many of the loopholes that allow this are being closed by the U.S. Department of Labor, others remain. The large pot of pension wealth is always subject to mismanagement, or worse. *It's your job to protect your interests.*

Retirement Plan Strategy No. 1: Educate Yourself about Your Existing Pension Plan

The first thing you need to do is to understand the type of pension plan you have. If you don't, get someone to explain it to you. If you work for a company, there is almost certainly a plan administrator who is responsible for understanding and explaining the details of the plan. If you have set up your own plan, then you need to speak with the individual who actually set it up, to go through all of your various options for contributing to the plan.

If you become convinced that *nobody* understands it, then you and your fellow employees should all chip in and hire a lawyer to look the plan over thoroughly. An expert's fee is a small amount of money compared to losing everything. If you ever get to this point, make sure you hire a lawyer who specializes in employment law and pension plans.

Find out where the pension plan's money is held. If all the company's pension money is invested in the company's own stock, that should be cause for concern, even if the stock is doing well at the moment. Does it make any sense to have all of the money in one stock? Just use common sense. Too much money in one basket is a recipe for disaster. That's precisely how so many Enron employees lost all (or nearly all) of their retirement funds: They were compelled to invest their money in Enron stock, and when that company imploded, the stock became worthless.

If the money isn't invested in the company's stock, where is it? Perhaps it's all sitting in a low-yielding money market account because no one is willing to take the risk of doing something else. This is bad stewardship, at best; the administrator of the company pension plan should be investing appropriately for *all* employees. Giving up returns out of laziness or insecurity is simply not acceptable.

> *No decision is difficult to make if you will get all of the facts.*
>
> —George S. Patton

Retirement Plan Strategy No. 2: Be Proactive with Your Retirement Money Manager

You should be an advocate for a well-diversified retirement plan, with a blend of types of investments and a range of styles of investing, from conservative to aggressive. Plan flexibility is extremely important, because your strategy is likely to change over time. The 20-year-old employee can afford to be more aggressive, but as you reach retirement age, you need to be more conservative than your twenty-something colleagues.

Find out who's managing your money. Is the manager churning the accounts aggressively (trading frequently in order to generate high fees) or does she or he have a more reasonable approach to investing? Remember, when no one's watching, your account is open to attack from both mismanagement and overtrading of the account to generate high fees. The easiest way to spot a potential problem is to see if there is a high turnover ratio in the investment portfolio, which is generating high fees for *someone*. As a rule, a high turnover ratio in the context of a retirement plan is difficult to justify. Make someone justify it to you.

At a minimum, make sure your company is following government guidelines for retirement accounts. For example, for all 401(k) accounts, the largest sector of retirement plans for employees, companies must follow the Department of Labor Rule 404(c) for administration of the plan. This rule calls for the following:

1. The company must offer at least three diversified investment options with different levels of risk.
2. Employees must be allowed to move money from one investment to another at least once every three months.
3. Participants must be provided with a prospectus and other educational material about each investing option.
4. Employees must receive investment education, so that they can understand the options provided to them.
5. Employers must offer reeducation of employees if conditions in the plan change.

Again, these are *minimum* standards. If you are not getting even these minimal kinds of assistance, something is wrong, and you need to find out what it is.

Make sure that you and your fellow employees get a statement of your account no less than quarterly to show the value of your account, where it is invested, and how you can direct a change if you feel one is necessary.

Retirement Plan Strategy No. 3: Take Your Retirement Money Seriously

For a lot of people, money that they haven't actually seen is play money. *That's the wrong attitude.* Instead, you need to treat your retirement nest egg like the precious commodity it is. These may be the only retirement dollars you'll ever see, and it may make a real difference in your retirement lifestyle.

Find out about your investing options, and make sure your money is always working the way you want it to. Adopting a good retirement plan is likely to require analyzing your investment options quarterly to see which one is likely to perform best based on the current state of the economy. If the economy changes, be strong enough to alter your investment options. Strive to be invested where you have the opportunity to earn the greatest amount of money.

Retirement Plan Strategy No. 4: Roll Over Your Company Retirement Plan into Your IRA

When you leave a company today, you generally have three options relating to your retirement plan:

1. Leave it where it is.
2. Roll it into your new company's retirement plan.
3. Roll the accumulated amount into your own IRA.

Option 3 is the best choice, because it gives you the greatest flexibility. If you roll your 401(k) into your IRA, the money will continue to grow tax-deferred, plus you will have more options as to where to invest the money than if you had left it where it was.

Also, if you roll the money into your own IRA, you (not your employer) have control over it. There is no good reason to keep your retirement money invested with your former employer. Even if the plan holds only company stock, you are better off holding that stock *yourself*, in your own IRA.

Rollover rules are pretty specific. If you elect to move your IRA, you must roll over (reinvest) the money within 60 days, or it will be considered a distribution to you of your retirement money. This means you will have to pay full income taxes on the amount received, plus a penalty of 10 percent for a premature distribution. This is a huge mistake; don't make it. Roll over any retirement money you have in a 401(k), 403(b), 457, or other such company plan into your IRA as soon as you can.

To conform to the 60-day time limit, use a direct rollover, which moves your money directly from one trustee to another without your taking possession. This is an automatic process, and because no money passes through your hands, there is no risk of a distribution and tax to you.

Retirement Plan Strategy No. 5: Use Self-Directed IRAs for Maximum Flexibility

Once you have rolled over your retirement plan into an IRA, make sure your IRA is *self-directed*. This means that your IRA allows you to make investments with as much flexibility as the law allows. This was a greater problem in the past than it is today. Banks, for example, were one of the biggest proponents of IRAs in the beginning. Yet, if you opened your IRA with a bank, you were extremely limited in your investment options. In many cases, all you could do was buy the bank's CDs or money-market funds.

While those restrictions have eased somewhat, you still need to make sure that your IRA allows you maximum flexibility in what you

Plans must be simple and flexible.

—George S. Patton

can invest in. If your trustee tells you that the plan lets you invest only in certain things, like the institution's own CDs, tell him or her good-bye and move your money elsewhere. There are too many other good options around.

Self-directed IRAs allow you to put your money into any investment that is not excluded by the government. This is plenty broad, for our purposes—although realtors still complain, because there are restrictions on the type of real estate you can invest in.

Good news usually comes with some strings attached, and self-directed IRAs are no exception. In this case, the strings come in the form of higher fees for administration, because the different investment options require more paperwork. To some extent, however, the administrative costs of regular IRAs have been subsidized by plan sponsors, who want to get IRA business in order to capture more than just IRA money. There is nothing inherently wrong with that approach, as long as you understand the process and make your decisions accordingly.

Retirement Plan Strategy No. 6: Be Proactive in Investing Your 401(k)

Your 401(k) retirement plan can perform only as well as the investment options you're given. The federal government requires your employer to give you three investment options, but if your employer chooses money market funds, the company's stock, and a bond fund, you are likely to lose out on big returns, unless you are lucky enough to work for a company with a soaring stock price that remains high. The other two options are conservative and may not take advantage of a growing market or even beat the rate of inflation.

In order to increase your potential, you (perhaps as part of a group of fellow employees) should speak to the company's retirement administrator and lobby for more investment options. Although this might seem to be a difficult task in a large company, you may find it much easier than you thought.

The best time to start thinking about your retirement is before the boss does.

—Anonymous

Remember, the plan administrator's retirement money is tied up in the same program as yours. By using real data on the returns on different sectors of the market, you may be able to demonstrate to his or her satisfaction the advantage of having multiple options.

At a minimum, your retirement plan should have the following options to maintain a good diversified investment mix:

1. *A money market fund.* This, as we explained in the last chapter, is simply a place to move your money when things get rough in the market.
2. *Three bond funds.* The company should offer a short-, a medium-, and a long-term bond fund. Depending on what is happening to interest rates, you can increase or decrease your investment exposure to fluctuation.
3. *An index fund.* A fund that matches the S&P 500 or Russell 2000 offers growth with broader diversification in the market. Good index funds also should have very low management fees.
4. *A growth fund with moderate risk.* This type of fund usually contains large-cap stocks and perhaps some

mid-caps. The lower in size you go, the greater the risk factor tends to be, and the more aggressive the strategy is.

5. *An aggressive growth fund.* These funds usually invest in small-cap stocks, which tend to be more volatile in their price swings. (This is why they are considered more aggressive.)

6. *A growth and income fund.* These funds try to offer a mix of stocks for growth and either bonds or preferred stock for income.

7. *The company's own stock.* This can be good news or bad. If your company's stock is doing well, great. But remember, overconcentration in any one investment can get you in a lot of trouble if things go bad. This was the problem experienced by all of those people who worked for the scandal-plagued companies of the early 2000s.

8. *An international fund.* Investing in companies that do business outside the United States gives you some diversity relative to our own economy.

These eight alternatives make up a solid core of investment options, which should cover you in a range of economic conditions. Other people (including your plan administrator) may disagree, but as we see it, this is the *minimum* acceptable number of options for a modern retirement plan.

In addition to increasing the number of selections available, you should encourage your retirement plan administrator to provide classes in smart investing, to help you and your fellow employees better understand these options and how to put them to use. Financial education for employees is now one of the requirements of the Employee Retirement Income Security Act of 1974 (ERISA), but sometimes an employer needs a gentle prod.

Retirement Plan Strategy No. 7: Know Your Retirement Plan Rights

You have a number of protections under ERISA, and in order to get their full benefit, you need to understand them well.

You have the right to examine all of the documents filed with the U.S. Department of Labor about your plan. Your plan administrator must provide this information to you without charge. You can also demand copies of these documents, although you may be charged a reasonable fee. But if you have to demand copies of your plan, there may be some kind of problem going on, and you should investigate further.

You are entitled to a copy of your retirement plan's annual financial report from the plan administrator.

You are entitled to receive, at any time, a statement of what benefits you would receive if you retired now. If you haven't vested in the retirement plan, the administrator must give you the rules and advise you how many more years you have before vesting.

As in law so in war, the longest purse finally wins.

—Mahatma Gandhi

Vesting, which is the period of time before you are allowed to keep as yours all the benefits that have been added to your plan by your employer, is a common provision used to attract and keep good employees. It should, however, be balanced so that the required period is not an unreasonable length of time.

You cannot be legally terminated by an employer in order to prevent you from getting your retirement benefits or exercising your rights.

Retirement Plan Strategy No. 8: Use IRA Plans to Your Best Advantage

Earlier, we discussed the benefits of rolling over company retirement plans into IRAs once you leave your company. There are several different kinds of IRAs to consider. A regular IRA provides you with tax deferral on your income, but you pay on distribution. A Roth IRA is not tax deductible, and you have to pay tax when you convert from your 401(k). Once you pay, however, you don't pay again, and the Roth IRA continues to grow tax-free forever.

Whether you're rolling over a company plan or creating a retirement fund of your own, IRAs can be a good investment tool. All "earned income" wage earners can set up a Roth IRA if their modified adjusted gross income does not exceed $95,000 (single) or $150,000 (married filing jointly). There is both a phase out and a cap on income above that. The maximum contribution for 2005 to 2007 is $4,000 per year. If you are over 55 years of age, you can contribute an additional $500 in 2005, $1,000 in 2006, and $1,000 in 2007, under a "catch-up" provision designed to help those closer to retirement beef up their investment accounts.

Retirement Plan Strategy No. 9: Convert Your Regular IRA to a Roth IRA

The primary benefit to the Roth IRA is that the money earned in the account is not taxed. Depending on your age, there may be substantial benefits to you from converting to the Roth IRA. If you use the Roth IRA as a long-term planning tool by passing it on to your heirs, then your heirs will have the benefit of longer compounding periods. In other words, using this strategy increases the number of years of tax-free compounding, and ultimately gives your beneficiaries more tax-free income.

Retirement Plan Strategy No. 10: Designate What Happens to Your IRA When You Die

Many people avoid thinking about their death. But if you have a family, you have a responsibility to think about unpleasant things. (It comes with the territory.) For example, you owe it to them to think about what happens to your IRA account if you die.

If you are married when you die, your spouse is automatically the beneficiary of your retirement plan, unless another beneficiary has been designated in writing. This may cause problems for separated spouses, so specifying a retirement plan distribution should be part of any divorce settlement.

If you are not married, you can designate anyone as a beneficiary, and you should list that person or persons in your plan, so that upon your death your IRA goes directly to that person without a court's intervention (i.e., probate). The individual receiving your IRA can then use the proceeds as her or his own IRA, subject to any distributions that may have already been made. This is a powerful way to build a large value for your heirs, as they continue to defer taxes in the IRA that you started, and it has more years to continue compounding instead of being closed and taxes being paid upon distribution (again, this pertains to a regular IRA, but not a Roth IRA).

Every person who has an IRA can (and should) name a specific individual to pass the IRA to directly, without its going through a will or probate. To do this, you must fill out a specific beneficiary form. If you don't complete the form, the beneficiary of your

IRA will be determined by state law or your will, and your IRA will be subject to estate claims and probate costs.

There is no reason to allow this to happen, and there is a large benefit from years of deferred compounding of tax-free (or tax-deferred) dollars to your heirs. All you need to do is fill out the beneficiary form. Do it!

Retirement Plan Strategy No. 11: Stretch Your IRA Generations for Maximum Wealth Building

An IRA can be used to build a legacy of wealth by stretching the inheritance among several generations. To maximize the effectiveness of compounding, your beneficiaries should be taught to use other money for their own needs and let the IRA continue to grow until they need it—or, if possible, *pass it to the next generation.*

This should also be a lesson to you: As a retirement plan owner, you should use other money you have before dipping into your IRA. You will have to take the required minimum distribution under the law based on the mortality tables, but assuming that you don't need the money, keeping the IRA as long as possible for your heirs is a great estate-planning opportunity.

To get maximum advantage from this generational deferral, IRAs should first be left to a spouse (if she or he needs the money).

> *The torch has been passed to a new generation.*
> —John Fitzgerald Kennedy

Then have the surviving spouse convert the IRA to a Roth IRA and name the next generation of children (or, better yet, grandchildren) as the beneficiaries of the IRA. Once the nonspouse beneficiary inherits, she or he can stretch distribution according to the life expectancy tables. Check current law at the time of selecting the beneficiary.

Retirement Plan Strategy No. 12: Learn the Rule of 72 to Plan Your Retirement

The rule of 72 is a quick way to calculate how long it will take for your investments, such as the ones in your IRA, to double, based on a certain yield. Understanding the rule helps you plan the amount of money you need to save for retirement.

To use the rule, take the number 72 and divide it by the percentage of interest you are earning on your investment. The answer is the number of years it will take for your money to double.

YEARS TO DOUBLE

Yield	6%	12%	15%	20%
Years to Double	72/6=12	72/12=6	72/15=4.8	72/20=3.6

Remember, in investments, time can work either for you or against you. Knowing the rules will help you understand how to make time work *for* you.

YOUR MISSION TO WEALTH TO-DO LIST

1. LEARN ABOUT YOUR EXISTING PENSION PLAN. Some pension plans are defined-benefit plans, meaning that you're guaranteed a certain level of benefits in retirement. IRAs, 401(k)s, and other similar plans are

defined-contribution plans, meaning that you (and maybe your employer) make a specific contribution to the plan. Understand what *you* have. Take it seriously— even if that money doesn't seem real yet. There will come a time (sooner than you think) when this money is going to be very real to you. Your job is to make sure that there's enough of it.

2. **IF NECESSARY, RESHAPE THAT PLAN.** No, your company isn't going to hand over direction of the pension plan to you. But if the options that your company provides to you are too limited, you probably can have an impact on expanding or changing those choices. Be proactive.

3. **WHEN APPROPRIATE, OR WHEN REQUIRED, ROLL OVER.** If you leave the company that's been providing you with a pension plan, take your money with you. Make sure that you reinvest that money within 60 days, or you will be subject to a whopping tax-and-penalty bite. Avoid this mistake at all costs!

4. **USE IRAS FOR CREATIVE ESTATE PLANNING.** One of the key lessons of this book is the *power of compounding*. The tax laws permit the passing on of IRAs to subsequent generations, which greatly increases the life of the IRA and the associated compounding of interest. Look into setting up your estate in such a way as to make this possible. Let people know that they should use this money only when necessary, and should pass it along when possible.

5. **UNDERSTAND HOW THE NUMBERS WORK.** Get a feel for how quickly your money will double at the interest rates that you're likely to earn. Some people actually make the mistake of squirreling away so much for the future that they deny themselves a happy life today. Don't be a grasshopper, but don't be an overly stingy ant, either. If it looks like you're on track for a comfortable retirement, make today comfortable, too.

★ ★ ★

CHAPTER 13

Invest in Your Child's Education

Resolve to perform what you ought; perform without fail what you resolve.

—Benjamin Franklin

No matter what the current ages of your children or grandchildren, it is never too soon to think about their futures, and how you can invest in their success. College tuition, in particular, is an investment that you need to start planning for well in advance.

All long-term financial planning, including plans to pay for college, requires that you know two key facts before you begin your "journey of accumulation": what you have now, and what you'll need at the targeted future date. The annual cost (tuition, room, board, and fees) of a public college or university in the United States currently begins at about $10,000.

For a private institution, the cost begins at $25,000 per year and goes up from there. Assuming that the cost of a college education will continue to rise at the rate of 8 to 10 percent per year, you can expect to pay at least $15,000 (and probably well more than that) for a year of public higher learning in another ten years, and over $40,000 per year at a private institution. (Note that some private colleges are already in the mid $30,000 range; these schools may cost twice that in ten years. And note that some recent estimates project the rate of "education inflation" to top *12 percent* in coming years.) Failure to plan for this large a financial event will result in either financial hardship or a "reduced" education, or both.

> *A child miseducated is a child lost.*
> —John Fitzgerald Kennedy

The key to success lies in getting an early start. If you begin a college investment account for your child the month he or she is born and deposit $250 per month into it, and if that account makes an average of 13 percent per year, you can have more than $200,000 accumulated by the time that child is ready to walk through the doorway of his or her dorm. If you do the same thing at the rate of $100 per month, you still will have more than $85,000 socked away by the time you send your son or daughter to college.

The lesson here is that you need to decide what kind of education you want to pay for and how much you can contribute. Perhaps you can't contribute anything like $250 per month, but you *can* manage $100 per month. If that's the case, then your child will have to go to an in-state public university, or he or she will have to qualify for scholarships or financial aid, or someone (you or your child) will have to take out education loans.

Education Investment Strategy No. 1: Avoid Savings Bonds and CDs for College Funding Vehicles

As noted earlier, some experts are projecting that "education inflation" may exceed 12 percent a year in the near future. You need to pay particularly close attention to this bit of data if you're considering using savings bonds or other "really safe" instruments as the primary vehicles to save for your children's college educations. The unpleasant fact is that there is *no way* you will be able to cover the cost of your child's college education, or even a significant portion thereof, if you use savings bonds, certificates of deposit, money market funds, or any other similar types of instruments that traditionally have been used for college savings.

Yes, these instruments are safe, and safety is important when it comes to saving for college. But they can't keep up with inflation. What good will safety do you if, in the end, it doesn't buy you the product you've been saving for?

> *Never send a battalion to take a hill if you've got a division.*
>
> —Dwight D. Eisenhower

Education Investment Strategy No. 2: Stick with Stock Mutual Funds

To have the best chance to amass the money you'll need, you need to invest in either individual stocks or stock mutual funds. We vote for stock mutual funds. They offer the benefits of market growth, while diminishing market risk through the diversification that is a natural part of the structure of a mutual fund.

The portfolio of a large mutual fund includes as many as 100 individual stocks. This means that while your mutual fund will be generally reflective of the movement of the stock market as a whole, it will not sink on the heels of the poor performance of just a few of the stocks contained in the portfolio.

In addition, because mutual funds are managed stock portfolios, you don't have to spend much time checking on them, making adjustments, and so on. So they are a low-maintenance funding choice like the savings bond or certificate of deposit, but they will deliver a far superior return over the long run.

Education Investment Strategy No. 3: Beware of Specialized "Invest for College" Programs

Many mutual fund companies now offer their own type of specialized college investment program that invests in a particular selection of their funds. When you call a fund company and say that you're looking to invest for college, you're likely to be directed to whatever program that fund company has in place for that purpose. Not knowing any better, many investors take the company's word and jump in, assuming that the fund company must know what it's doing and that its designated college investment program *must* be the best way to go.

Remember, though, that mutual fund college programs exist primarily as a marketing tool, so that the fund company can say that it has a specialized program for college investors. There is nothing inherently wrong with this, but many of these programs are too conservative to reach your goal. They may well be stock mutual funds, but they are usually among the most conservative of the company's stock fund offerings.

If you are beginning your college investment plan for your child while she or he is still very young, you will have somewhere between 10 and 18 years to let the money remain invested. With that time frame, you should have little hesitancy about selecting a solid array of growth mutual funds into which your regular college savings should be placed.

The point of longer-term investing goals is to get a diversified portfolio that offers upside potential. You should be more aggressive in the early years, so that if the market stumbles, your fund has time to recover. As your child gets closer to college age, you can start shifting to a more conservative strategy.

Education Investment Strategy No. 4: Avoid the Outdated UGMA Account Umbrella

Until recently, the Uniform Gifts to Minors Act (UGMA) largely determined how you should invest for a child's education expenses. The tax benefit of the UGMA investment account is that the first $750 of annual investment income earned is tax free, while the second $750 (these amounts are indexed to inflation, and therefore are adjusted upward periodically) is taxed at the child's tax rate. Any earnings that exceed $1,500 are taxed at the adult custodian's rate, which is higher.

UGMA accounts have three problems. First, they're not competitive with more recent types of savings accounts. (See the next section.) Second, because the UGMA account is in the name of the minor child, the account comes under the child's control when he or she reaches the age of majority. (This varies by state, but the age is typically 18.) What can the custodial parent do if, on his or her eighteenth birthday, the young person, who now controls the account, decides to spend all that money on a new car, instead of using it to pay educational expenses? Nothing.

The third problem with these accounts has to do with college financial aid formulas. In general, colleges take the position that roughly one-third of any monies belonging to the student are regarded as being available to meet college expenses, while less than 6 percent of parents' monies are considered to be available. As a result, the more money that is held in the child's name, the less the financial aid that the child will be eligible to receive.

Education Investment Strategy No. 5: Use 529 Plans and Coverdale Savings Accounts

Today, the best options are state-sponsored college savings plans, referred to as 529 plans, and the Coverdale Savings Account, also known as an education IRA. While there is some variance in features between the two plans, the most important advantage of each is that it is essentially tax free to you.

The 529 is a state-sponsored plan, and because of that, it can be a little restrictive. Under the terms of this plan, the state selects a particular brokerage or investment company with which you may open an account. In some states, you have a choice of investment options for the money you contribute to the plan; in other states, there is a manager who makes all the decisions for you. In some states, contributions can be tax-deductible, while this is not true in other states. (Find out the specific rules in your state.)

The unique advantage of the 529 plan is the huge sums of money that can be contributed to it. Unlike the Coverdale account, which has a current annual contribution limit of $2,000, you can contribute $50,000 or more in one year to the 529 (although there is a lifetime contribution limit, which varies by state). This feature is particularly important to people who have the means and the resolve to make a serious dent in the future cost of their children's educational costs.

As for the Coverdale Savings Plan (also known as the education IRA), this is a purely private college investment account. You are not restricted as to where you set up the account, and you may invest your contributions in whatever investment choices your custodian offers—obviously an attractive feature as you become a more and more sophisticated investor over time.

The bottom line is that with 529s and Coverdales, you have two excellent account umbrellas from which to choose. Both types of account allow your money to grow tax-deferred, and if the money is withdrawn and provably used for college expenses, it remains untaxed at withdrawal, which means that these are basically tax-free accounts.

It is more important to do what is right than to do what is personally beneficial.

—Colin Powell

Also, in the calculation of financial aid, these accounts are considered *parental* assets, so your child may qualify for more financial aid.

So, if you are in a position to contribute substantially more than $2,000 per year to your child's college investment account, opt for the 529 plan (but do your homework and look for a good one). If not, then choose the Coverdale, which will give you much more flexibility as to where you open the account, as well as to the number and breadth of investment choices you'll have.

One more thing: There are income limits that affect one's eligibility to contribute to a Coverdale, but they're high. Still, if you're married and file jointly, your ability to contribute to a Coverdale begins to phase out if you earn $190,000 per year ($95,000 if you're single). Granted, it's a nice problem to have. And if you have it, you will also want to look at the 529.

Education Investment Strategy No. 6: Consider State Prepaid Tuition Plans

Now we have to introduce yet another choice: the state prepaid tuition plan. Although the 529 plan is a product of the state, and although 529s are sometimes referred to as "529 prepaid tuition plans," the true prepaid plan is something different. With a prepaid tuition plan, you lock in the future cost of a college education by purchasing chunks, or *contracts*, of tuition at today's rates.

The basic premise of the prepaid tuition plan is sound, but you must examine your state's version closely before you opt for one over a 529 plan, for example. Prepaid tuition plans were originally designed so that they could be used *only* to pay for in-state public universities and colleges. In the interest of competition, many states have since changed their plans so that they can also be used at out-of-state institutions and at private colleges and universities. But remember that *each state's plan is different*, and before you sign up, know what you're getting into.

In general, the prepaid tuition plan is probably a good option if you know that you want your child to attend a state college or university *and* you don't have the means to contribute substantial sums to a 529. In that situation, a prepaid plan may be the best choice.

Education Investment Strategy No. 7: Look into All Scholarship Options

What comes to your mind when you envision the winner of a college scholarship or similar grant? Do you think, for example, of a highly rated high school athlete, a super-smart student, a member of a minority group, or someone from a poor family?

If so, think again. The fact is that *most* scholarships and grants do not have any of these factors as criteria for eligibility. There are literally thousands of groups and organizations in this country that offer everything from small grants to full four-year college scholarships, and yet few among us have any clue that this is the case. Many people forgo a college education simply because they don't know about the assistance they qualify for.

Don't make this mistake. Don't automatically take your student out of the scholarship race. When the time comes, talk with your child's high school counselor and with college finan-cial aid officers to see what is available. You may be pleasantly surprised.

A word of caution: A number of scholarship-search companies have been set up in recent years, aimed at bringing together eligible students with scholarship funding. For the most part, these are for-profit companies, and they serve a useful and legitimate purpose. But if any such firm asks you for a large up-front payment, be wary. If you think the company is not entirely on the up and up, check with your state attorney general's office to see if any complaints have been lodged against the company.

NEW COLLEGE OPTIONS

The next few sections are aimed equally at the parent (or other fam-ily member) who is paying for the education and the student who is getting educated. They involve basic choices about the *kind* of education the student is going to receive.

Nothing is constant except change. As society moves forward, it finds new ways of doing just about everything. Getting a college degree is one thing that certainly falls into that category. By the time your younger children reach college, the typical college experience may have changed dramatically.

Until recently, most of us felt that in order to receive a college degree, we had to live the "classic" college existence of residing at a school (or at least commuting to it every day) and sitting in a class-room. That is no longer the case. Now, more and more colleges and universities are offering a "virtual" learning experience to "distance learners." Simply put, this means taking online courses and studying on one's own, with limited interactions with both faculty and fellow students.

There are several significant advantages to attending college this way. First, the cost is considerably lower, because the student is not using the campus facilities, staff, and other resources. Second, most virtual students have much greater latitude in terms of when and how they complete their studies. Distance learning students are normally permitted to complete their studies at their own pace, which most traditional students don't get to do.

I am always ready to learn, but I do not always like being taught.

—Winston Churchill

At the same time, there are some clear disadvantages to studying this way. For one thing, the classroom dynamic is missing. All the extracurricular elements and the intangibles of a college education (athletics, clubs, social life) are also unavailable to the virtual learner. In addition, distance learners without sufficient self-discipline may find it difficult to buckle down and complete their work, since no one is looking over their shoulders. For these and other reasons, you should assume that the distance learner won't get the whole college experience.

Again, you choose the distance-learning route to save money and gain flexibility. If you don't have any other good choices, you shouldn't feel bad about choosing this one. Make certain, though, that if you pursue the virtual college or distance-learning option, you do so with a legitimate, *accredited* college or university. Beware of the unaccredited diploma mills that dispense "degrees" in exchange for money. The best way to deal with this issue is to stick with well-known schools that primarily offer a traditional, campus-oriented education but that have added the opportunity to pursue a degree via distance or Internet learning. In these cases, accreditation should not be an issue.

Education Investment Strategy No. 8: Consider a Military Option for College Education

Service in the U.S. military is an excellent way to secure a college education. While many people are initially reluctant to consider this option, there are a variety of reasons to take it seriously. First, there's a *lot* of money available through the military for college. In fact, the military is the largest source of college "scholarship" money, other than low-income aid programs.

Service in the military strengthens one's résumé. Additionally, the military experience is one that most people find to be positive, as it provides opportunities for worldwide travel and unique experiences and challenges that are hard to come by in the civilian world.

There are basically two ways to get money for college through military service. One way is to first serve as an enlisted person and then receive your money afterward, much in the style of the old GI Bill. This is a good option for people who are not necessarily looking for a career in the military but are willing to do a few years of military service after high school in exchange for the tremendous benefit of being able to attend college debt free after their service. Each branch of the service offers its own version of this opportunity, so you'll want to talk to a recruiter from each branch to see just what is available and how one particular opportunity might be the best fit for you or your child.

Here's something else to consider: Each branch of the military normally gives enlistment bonuses to people who select certain job specialties and/or lengths of enlistments when they go in. These bonuses, which can be as high as $20,000, are separate from any college funding monies that may be doled out later. So someone who is careful to take his or her time and investigate all the options may be able to receive a considerable sum of money that can be applied to college once the enlistment is up.

You cannot push anyone up a ladder unless he is willing to climb himself.

—Andrew Carnegie

The other way to pay for a college education through military service is by attending college first on the military's dime, then repaying Uncle Sam through several years of service following graduation. These kinds of programs differ significantly from those previously discussed, in that the student, upon graduation, also receives a commission as an officer in his or her selected branch of the service.

Attendance at a federal academy is perhaps the best known of these opportunities. As a student at the U.S. Military Academy (West Point), Naval Academy (Annapolis), Air Force Academy, Coast Guard Academy, or Merchant Marine Academy, a young person can receive one of the very best educations available anywhere, *for free.*

Getting into one of the five service academies requires both a competitive test score and a congressional appointment, which can be difficult to get. In addition, the four years spent at these places are *highly* demanding and have little in common with civilian colleges and universities. Life at the federal academies is not for everyone. And, of course, there is a service obligation following graduation.

On the other hand, the academies strive for geographic distribution and are always looking for athletes for their sports teams (male and female), so don't assume that your child *can't* get an appointment. The Merchant Marine Academy at Kings Point, New York, is less well known than the other academies, meaning that an appointment may be easier to come by. All five academies offer strong engineering programs, among other degree options, and can open up an amazing range of career opportunities.

For people who would rather pursue this type of military option through a regular college or university, there is the ROTC (Reserve

Officer Training Corps) option. Many high-quality colleges and universities have ROTC departments on campus, and each branch of the military makes ROTC opportunities available. By enrolling in ROTC, a student attends classes and lives the life of every other student on campus, with a few exceptions.

The ROTC student takes some extra classes in military science, leadership, and other areas that are germane to the proper training of a future officer in the U.S. military. Weekends and summers are usually spent in military training. Upon graduation, the student receives not only a degree but also a commission in his or her chosen branch of the military.

Only those who dare to fail greatly can ever achieve greatly.
—Robert F. Kennedy

As for the financial benefits of ROTC, there are different terms of ROTC scholarships that cover two to four years of college expenses. Four-year ROTC scholarships are the most difficult to secure, but there are plenty of opportunities to earn smaller sums of money through ROTC, and the amounts are still significant. To learn more about the ROTC opportunities available through each branch of the military, contact Air Force ROTC at www.afoats.af.mil, Army ROTC at www.tradoc.army.mil/rotc/index.html, and Navy/Marine Corps ROTC at www.cnet.navy.mil.

Education Investment Strategy No. 9: Consider Community College for the First Two Years

One of the best ways to get an affordable college education today is to complete two years at a local community college. The first two years of a bachelor's degree education are basically spent working at core courses and prerequisite courses. These studies can be pursued at a community college just as easily, and much more cheaply, than at a four-year institution.

No, attending community college isn't as glamorous as going to a big-name university, but who cares? No one is concerned about where you spent the first two years of college. What's more, the community college option offers the advantage of allowing you to earn an associate's degree while completing your core course requirements, which is something you can't do at most four-year schools.

Another good reason to go the community college route is that it is an excellent way for your child to make the transition into the world of higher education without having to deal with the added pressures and temptations associated with living away from home. We all know of people who went off to college and flunked out because they could not handle their new situation. This is a waste of hard-earned money, and it also sullies an academic record to such a degree that it's often difficult for such a person to properly restart his or her education.

And as long as we're on the subject: Parents who are about to send a child off to college should *seriously consider* tuition insurance. This is likely to be offered to you by the college, through a private provider. (If it isn't, ask.) It's extremely cheap, and it qualifies you for either complete or partial tuition reimbursement if your student can't finish a semester.

Education Investment Strategy No. 10: Go to School Part-Time

One of the easiest ways to deal with the cost of college is to attend on a part-time basis. Again, some people have a problem with this, as it detracts from the overall experience. However, you do what you have to do to deal with the economic realities of life, including the very real problem of rising college costs.

Other than the fact that it will obviously take you longer to earn your degree if you attend part time, there isn't really any disadvantage to this strategy. Meanwhile, there are two very real advantages. First, of course, you can make money to help pay for school. And second, you can create an employment history and gain real-world skills and knowledge in a way that you can't do as a full-time student.

You should remember, though, that in order to maximize this opportunity, the time that you spend working should be in a job that has some relevance to your chosen field of study. If you spend your time busing tables or working

Experience is something you get too late to do anything about the mistakes you made while getting it.
—Anonymous

as a salesperson in a stereo store, or doing some other job that has little relevance to your studies, it won't do much for your résumé.

YOUR MISSION TO WEALTH TO-DO LIST

1. **FIGURE OUT WHAT YOU NEED.** The cost of both public and private education is skyrocketing. Your starting point should be (a) how much do I have now, (b) how much will I need, and (c) how will I close whatever gap exists?

2. **STAY AWAY FROM LOW-YIELD INSTRUMENTS.** The traditional "safe" vehicles—certificates of deposit, savings bonds, and so on—simply won't get you there. Instead, go with stock mutual funds. These have higher

risk and more volatility, but at least they have a *chance* of helping you hit your target.

3. SAY NO TO UGMA, YES TO 529 AND COVERDALE. Accounts set up under the Uniform Gifts to Minors Act have major weaknesses. Investigate alternatives like 529 plans and Coverdale accounts.

4. INVESTIGATE STATE PREPAID TUITION PROGRAMS. These plans have become more flexible in recent years, allowing (in many cases) for out-of-state schooling. Check the specifics of your state's plan.

5. ASSUME THAT YOUR CHILD IS ELIGIBLE FOR SCHOLAR-SHIP ASSISTANCE. Chances are that there's money out there. Find it, with help from high school guidance counselors, college financial aid officers, or specialized search firms.

6. CONSIDER ALTERNATIVES, INCLUDING MILITARY OPTIONS. There's nothing that says that you have to go to school full-time, or spend four years at a particular school, or even spend time on a campus at all. Consider *all* the options. Many of the better options involve letting Uncle Sam pay most or all of the freight.

★ ★ ★

CHAPTER 14

Insuring Your Financial Future

*We never prepared any battle plan without at
least one alternate plan.*

—Porter B. Williamson

Y ou can't build wealth in any meaningful way unless you have a
plan to *protect* your money once you've earned it. The more
money you make, the more likely it is that someone will try to take
it away from you.

The number one asset protector (and true wealth saver) is insurance. In this chapter, we'll look at lots of different kinds of insurance. Obviously, we can't cover all you need to know about *every*
type of insurance. What we *can* do is focus on what you need to
know, and blow away some of the smoke and fog that typically sur-
rounds the field of insurance.

HEALTH INSURANCE IS A MUST-HAVE

We start our review of insurance with the one that you simply have to have: *health insurance.*

We live in the richest country in the world. And yet, the United States has become a country of haves and have-nots in the area of health care. If you don't have insurance, you are one hospital visit away from financial disaster. You may survive your health crisis, only to find creditors pounding at your door. No, this isn't right, but it is reality—and you'd better get coverage.

Insurance Strategy No. 1: Join an Association If You Don't Have a Company Health Plan

One of the biggest benefits employees may get from their company is access to health-care coverage. If you are self-employed, or if you work for a company that doesn't offer health insurance coverage, then your best option is to join an association that does.

For instance, the National Association for the Self-Employed (www.NASE.org) provides group health insurance for its members. Rates may be higher than those for most company plans, but they are likely to be lower than anything you could get on your own. Coverage can be similar to company plans, but it really depends on the particular association's size and objectives.

If you are over 50, you may qualify for plans offered by the American Association for Retired People (www.aarp.org). Also, you can join the American Automobile Association (www.aaa.com) and get both you *and* your car covered (with different types of insurance).

Here are some things to look for when getting health insurance on your own:

1. *Coverage should be at least 80 percent* of both your hospital and other medical payments after you reach your deductible. (A *deductible* is simply the amount you agree to pay *before* the insurer has to start paying.) You may want more coverage, but this will be one of those trade-offs between more coverage and more cost.

2. *Out-of-pocket copayments should be capped at $2,000.* Don't be seduced by low premiums that hinge on huge copayments.

3. *Make sure the insurance has a guaranteed renewal provision* as long as you keep making the payments. You don't want to get sick and have your insurance cancelled.

4. *Find a plan that excludes exceptions for preexisting conditions.* Sometimes you just don't know you have a condition, and you don't want to battle the insurance company on whether something was or was not preexisting.

Insurance Strategy No. 2: Raise Your Deductible to Reduce Your Rates

Health insurance costs about 40 percent less if you agree to a $1,000 deductible instead of a $250 deductible. It's true that by raising your deductible, you shift some of the risk from the insurance company to you. And while you may have to pay some or all of the deductible if you become ill, you will actually come out ahead with lower premiums if you are and remain in good health.

Insurance Strategy No. 3: Get COBRA Health Coverage If You Leave Your Job

If you leave a job that has a health insurance plan, you will have to either get your own health coverage or find a job at another company that offers a plan (unless you can get coverage from your spouse or partner's company). Having to pay for your own policy will cost you more money, so hopefully your new employer will have a good plan. If it doesn't, seek coverage under COBRA (the federal Consolidated Omnibus Budget Reconciliation Act).

By law, COBRA allows you to stay on your old employer's health insurance plan for up to 18 months (and, under special circumstances, somewhat longer). You will pay the full cost of your health coverage yourself, but because you are still on the company plan, your benefits are likely to be better (and your premiums lower) than you can get on your own. In addition, COBRA also offers coverage for a spouse and dependent children should an insured spouse die.

To be prepared for war is one of the most effectual means of preserving peace.

—George Washington

So COBRA is there as an interim safety net. Be aware, though, that you have only a small time window in which to request coverage under COBRA, so act quickly. Contact your company's human resources department to get the appropriate forms, and fill them out so that you can qualify for coverage.

GET THE BEST INSURANCE ON YOUR HOME

Health insurance is the most critical type of insurance, but you also need to protect your home, your possessions, and yourself (against liability for accidents that happen in your residence). Your home is likely to be your most valuable asset, and you need to make sure it is covered.

You may not realize it, but you need insurance whether you own or rent your home. If you are currently renting a property, none of your possessions are protected by the owner's insurance, nor do you have liability protection. You need a separate tenant's insurance policy to protect you. These are relatively cheap. Get one today!

Insurance Strategy No. 4: Get 100 Percent Replacement Value Insurance on Your Home

You should always insure 100 percent of the replacement value of your home, even if that is more than your lender requires. Replacement value is more expensive than just coverage for the simple value of your home, because the term *replacement* protects you as costs go up. There is a big difference between the *depreciated* value of your home (which takes into account wear and tear) and the *replacement* value, which covers the full cost of rebuilding.

In addition to buying coverage for replacement value, some insurance companies require you to pay for an inflation rider to the insurance policy. This is further protection against rising cost of building materials.

While some people try to fudge a little on getting enough insurance coverage by putting a lower value on their home, this is not smart. Most insurance companies have a provision in their policies requiring you to insure your property for at least 80 percent of its replacement value. If you don't follow that rule and later make a claim, your insurers will automatically consider you underinsured, and reimburse you for only the actual depreciated value. This could really hurt in the event of major damage to your home.

Insurance Strategy No. 5: Get Additional Homeowner's Insurance Coverage

It's important to realize that the typical homeowner's insurance policy does not cover every disaster that could strike your home. In most cases, floods, hurricanes, earthquakes, and sinkholes (for example) require extra coverage, which you need to add to your regular homeowner's insurance policy. You should price out these optional coverages, based on where you live. For instance, Californians might decide that they need earthquake insurance, while homeowners living near a river might need flood insurance.

Get the coverage you need. If you are concerned about the additional cost of an extra policy, you can always increase your deductible. Insurance is always a balancing act between how much you can afford in premiums and how much loss you could stand to take. There is no "one size fits all," and your calculations are likely to change, the more money you make.

FIVE HOMEOWNER'S SUPER SAVERS

1. Combine your homeowner's insurance with the same insurance company you get auto insurance from, and get a multirated discount.
2. Raise your deductible to decrease cost, and become more "self-insured" to a modest extent. (Make sure you have enough money in savings to cover any deductibles.)
3. Ask for senior discounts, nonsmoker discounts, and discounts for security devices.
4. Consider eliminating expensive floater insurance for personal items, unless (a) you have a particular piece you

are concerned about and (b) you have a solid appraisal of the value of the item.

5. Make sure you insure only the *value of your home,* excluding land value.

INSURANCE FOR THE MANY ASPECTS OF YOUR LIFE

Health and homeowner's insurance are crucial in today's world. But, let's face it: No one likes to talk about life insurance. Talking to a salesman and then having to get a medical exam isn't much fun, but neither is the condition you will leave your heirs in if you don't have it. And it is the "when you need it" phrase that starts our learning point on life insurance.

Life insurance is intended to replace the income that you would otherwise have provided to your family. If you have young children and are the only (or primary) income-generating adult in your family, you *definitely* need life insurance, because your family most likely would experience a severe financial hardship if you passed away. On the other hand, if both spouses work and there are no minor children, your family probably needs less protection.

As with other forms of insurance, there are trade-offs between the amount of coverage you need and the premiums you pay for that coverage. So you need to think carefully

Good men must die, but death cannot kill their names.
—Spanish proverb

about what kind of insurance to get, how much to get, and how much you should expect to pay—all in relation to how much risk you're willing to bear versus the premium cost you are willing to pay.

Life insurance is confusing mainly because there are so many types to consider. This is compounded by the fact that it is sold by insurance companies, whose interests are not the same as yours. They are in business to make money, and it is in their best interest for you to buy the least and pay the most. This is not a dig at the insurance companies; it's just reality. The insurance industry is there to make money and give you protection. It is your responsibility to figure out what is best for you, financially.

There are several types of life insurance, and various subcategories within those types.

Insurance Strategy No. 6: Buy Term Insurance for Lowest-Cost Coverage

Term insurance provides life insurance for a specific period of time (the *term*). You pay a premium (monthly, quarterly, or annually) that's based on your age and health. The policy commits the insurance company to make a specific payment to your beneficiary if you die within that time period. If you do not die, you lose what you've paid on the insurance—but, of course, you have *gained*, because you are still living.

There are three types of term insurance:

1. *Annual renewable term.* This is a type of insurance that increases your premium the older you get (because your chance of staying alive decreases).
2. *Level term.* This is an insurance policy for a certain period of years, during which the premium remains the same.
3. *Decreasing term.* This is a form of term insurance where the premium remains the same but the promised insurance payout decreases.

Insurance Strategy No. 7: Use Permanent Insurance for Investment Options

The second major category of insurance is called *permanent* insurance. Like term, it also has three subcategories:

1. *Whole life.* This provides permanent protection for your entire life and gives you a specific insurance amount at a fixed rate and a future build-up of cash value within the policy. In other words, if you cancel the policy after a number of years have gone by, and you haven't borrowed against the policy, you may wind up with a cash payment.

2. *Universal life.* This combines the benefits of whole life with a lower starting premium, based on the assumption that the insurance company will make more on the investment of your premium. If it doesn't, however, your premium will rise in later years.

3. *Variable life.* This is similar to a universal policy, but it allows you to invest the premiums within the plan. If you invest well, you will profit. If you don't, you will pay higher premiums.

Permanent insurance is more expensive because you aren't just buying pure insurance; you're also paying the insurance company to set aside a portion of the premiums you pay to build a cash value for the future. But the reality of the situation is that the insurance company is investing the premium difference and giving you only *part* of the return. (It keeps the rest.) If you are comfortable making your own investments, you are better off buying term insurance and investing the premium savings in your own investment account.

Insurance Strategy No. 8: Don't Buy Decreasing Term Credit Life

Decreasing term policies are offered when you get your mortgage (mortgage life) or borrow money on a car (credit life). We looked at credit life in Chapter 9, "Cars: How to Drive a Real Bargain." You pay the same amount every month, but the insurance coverage decreases as the loan is paid off. When you make your last mortgage and insurance payment, you are paying a very big percentage to secure the small amount of insurance coverage of the last payment of your mortgage. This generates a high profit for the insurance company, but it's a bad insurance value for you.

A better way to provide for insurance coverage to pay off your loans should you die is to get a regular term insurance policy for the full value of the debt. A regular term life insurance policy will have the same premium and payout for the life of the policy. Should you die, your beneficiary would get the amount of your total original loan, not just the decreased amount based on how much you had paid down.

Insurance Strategy No. 9: Choose the Best Kind of Life Insurance for You

Maybe you already have some type of life insurance. If so, you should still ask yourself whether you have the right kind, and whether you have enough.

When you first bought your insurance, it is likely that your financial situation was different from what it is today. Today, you may need more, or you may need less. You may just need to adjust the type. Your strategy should be to (1) review what you have now and (2) review it again any time a major event occurs in your life (such as a birth or death or a major purchase like a home).

In our case, we both have term policies on our lives. We use life insurance for the specific reason it was created: income protection. In our cases, and even with our age differences, we both have chosen term life insurance with constant payment amounts and with different term periods.

We chose to make our investments separately and not within the insurance policy. We felt that we could make more money on our own investment programs than we could get from the insurance companies, so we chose to invest the difference in premiums ourselves. Is that right for you? Only if you also make investments on your own and if you can do better than the insurance companies.

If you *do* decide to buy permanent life, look *very carefully* at the quality of the insurance company. You won't build up any cash value if the company flounders or goes under.

Insurance Strategy No. 10: Never Cancel a Policy until a New One Is in Force

If you decide that your current policy isn't right for you, make sure that you don't cancel it until your new policy is paid for and in force. You aren't covered by the new policy until all of the contingencies are met. (Ask your broker exactly what they are and when they will be met.) You do *not* want a lapse in coverage. Keep your old plan in force until you are sure that the new one has become effective.

Insurance Strategy No. 11: Buy Disability Insurance

Most people don't buy disability insurance because of its expense. The reason it is expensive is that insurance companies have a larger chance of paying out on a disability contract than on other forms of insurance, and they price the insurance according to their risk.

But let's think about that. The point of insurance is to avoid a disaster. While you might be able to keep your household running for a month or longer if you become disabled, could you really keep things going for an extended period of time? How about for six months or more?

Don't let adverse facts stand in the way of a good decision.

—Colin Powell

The truth about disability insurance is that *you need it,* even if you think you don't. But getting what you need is not as easy, again because of the wide variety of policies that are out there and the varying definitions of coverage.

For example, the definition of disability is often a key question when determining which disability policy to buy. Standard contracts, which are cheaper, stipulate that the disability must make the policyholder unable to perform any occupation for which he or she has experience. Under this definition, a brain surgeon whose injured hand prevents him or her from performing brain surgery *isn't* disabled, assuming that he or she can still do other kinds of medical work.

In order to get adequate protection in this case, the doctor might want to pay for a more expensive policy—one that would pay if the doctor became unable to perform the duties of his specific occupation (brain surgery, in our example).

The waiting period is also important in determining how costly a policy is to buy. Why? Because the longer you agree to wait for disability coverage to kick in, the more likely it is that modern medicine will get you back on your feet. This means it is less likely that the insurance company will have to pay anything, so the premium will be lower. A waiting period of 90 days before the benefits begin is generally considered a good cost-versus-coverage option.

Five Years or Life—the Coverage Issue

How long should your disability coverage last? This is another question that has to be answered by weighing the known cost against the potential benefits. Certainly five years seems like a long time for protection, but *will* it be, if you have young children and your disability lingers? If you don't have longer coverage and you can't work in Year 6, what effect will this have on your family?

Finally, the *determination of disability* is an important consideration in picking a plan. In other words, who decides whether you are disabled, and how severely? If *your* doctor decides, the outcome may be more favorable to you than if the insurance company's doctor decides. This is clearly an issue that you want to check ahead of time.

So there's lots to sift through. How about a plan that covers a partial disability? Is that something you'd pay extra for? Once again, our advice is to go *shopping*. Figure out what's best for you, and find that coverage at a good price.

Deducting Premiums Could Cost You Money

If you own your own business and it pays your disability insurance premium, you can deduct the cost of the insurance as a business expense and save on taxes.

That may sound very appealing. Unfortunately, this tax savings could come back to haunt you, since any money you received on a claim would be considered taxable income. If, on the other hand, you paid your premium in after-tax dollars, then any payment you collected on a claim would be classified as an insurance payment and not subject to income tax. This would *substantially increase* your net benefit payment.

Insurance Strategy No. 12: Buy Long-Term Care Protection

Long-term care (LTC) insurance is the newest kind of insurance that requires a significant decision on your part. Because of medical advances, we are living longer. Statistically speaking, some of that additional time may well require a stay in some type of medical facility—and at a price that is escalating faster than your savings. To protect against that, consider long-term care insurance.

Age is the most important factor in determining the cost of long-term care. The younger you are when you start paying for an LTC policy, the longer you are likely to pay premiums before collecting on it, so your premiums will be lower.

As a rule of thumb, it is generally considered that cost-versus-coverage risk for LTC policies evens out at around the age of 50 to 55. Waiting longer increases the chances of needing coverage but being unable to buy it because you are sick and can't qualify. If you are 50, you can get a good plan for about $150 per month. If you wait until you are 70, you might pay $400 per month for a plan, if you can get it.

The bottom line is that if you are older than 55, you should buy long-term care insurance. While it may strike you as an unnecessary expense today, the chances are good that it will save you money in the long run. But, as with disability insurance, not all coverage is the same. It definitely pays to *read the fine print* of any policy you are considering before you buy it.

FIVE THINGS YOU MUST KNOW ABOUT LONG-TERM CARE COVERAGE

1. *How long you are covered for.* People don't generally stay in a nursing home for more than a couple of years, because either they go home or they die in the facility. But extended care is critical, because of the financial and emotional drain your family may experience in its absence. Five or six years is the minimum coverage you should consider.

2. *How long before coverage starts.* You can generally afford to be more flexible here. As with disability insurance, 90 days of self-insurance is about where you have the best cost-versus-benefit ratio.

3. *Who decides when you need care.* Just as with your disability policy, you want to avoid letting the insurance company determine when your coverage begins. Push to have your own doctor decide. If the company won't agree to that, push to have the decision made by a third party that has at least some degree of independence from the insurance company.

4. *Whether there is home-care coverage.* This type of option is an important consideration, especially if it is likely that you or a loved one would rather stay at home and get help

with care instead of going into a facility. You should get coverage that pays about as much as if you went into a facility, because the cost of home care is not much less, even though it is conducted in your own home.

5. *Whether there is inflation protection.* Even if inflation protection is offered only as a rider, you should consider it, because medical costs are rising faster than inflation, and it is unlikely that that trend will slow. You definitely don't want to find that your real benefits have been substantially reduced over the years because of rising costs.

Insurance Strategy No. 13: Do Not Rely on Medicare

Medicare is the insurer of last resort for people who need long-term care. It is an important benefit that is provided by our tax dollars, but whether it will always be there is something no one can tell. Counting on it as an insurance policy is not the best approach to long-term care.

The harsh reality is that even if Medicare exists by the time you need it (not a sure thing!), you will have to give up essentially *all* of your assets to get Medicare coverage. There are very strict laws on hiding or giving away assets to heirs in order to qualify, which further diminishes the appeal of Medicare.

We like to think of Medicare in the way it was intended to be thought of, back when it was created: as a safety net if all else fails. You'll get care if you have no other option, but it is your responsibility to plan ahead and get other coverage that will protect you better.

SAVE MONEY ON AUTO INSURANCE

While car insurance may seem like a mundane subject after a discussion of long-term care, getting the right auto insurance is critical to your financial well-being. So how do you do that?

Insurance Strategy No. 14: Get All the Discounts You Qualify For

Insurance companies, like most good businesses, reward people who are loyal. This means that if you have more than one car to insure, you will get a better break if you get the insurance on each one from the same company. If you can throw in your homeowner's insurance to make an even more attractive package, well, that's even better, and you probably will be rewarded with another discount.

Safe drivers are also favored by insurance companies. If you don't have any speeding tickets, ask for the discounts that almost all insurers have for safe drivers. Older drivers usually get better insurance deals than young people. Like the other discounts we mentioned, these are almost always available, but you must ask for them or you won't get them.

Sometimes one pays most for things one gets for nothing.

—Albert Einstein

Other factors that might qualify you for a discount:

★ Completion of a driver education course
★ A lack of prior accident claims
★ Antilock brakes
★ A car security system
★ Airbags

★ Being a "low-miles" driver

★ Garaging your car in the suburbs rather than the city

Insurance Strategy No. 15: Check the Insurance Ratings before You Buy a Car

Not all cars are created equal in the insurance world, so you may want to check with your carrier even before you buy. Higher-priced cars, bigger engines, how attractive the model is to thieves (think Corvette), and how the car stacks up in a safety test will all have an effect on the amount you pay.

Insurance Strategy No. 16: Purchase Auto Liability Insurance

If you have to cut back on your insurance costs, do it in places other than the liability component of your auto insurance.

Liability insurance protects you from injuries you cause to people in other cars, pedestrians, and passengers riding with you. It is generally quoted in two parts, like $100,000/$300,000. The first part is the maximum coverage per person, and the second is the maximum coverage per accident, if more than one person is injured. How much you need depends, in part, on how much you are worth (or *appear* to be worth). If you have considerable assets, you need more coverage in order to protect yourself.

Property damage liability is also important, because it pays for damage to other people's property if you are found to be at fault in an accident. Don't think you can skip it on the assumption that you aren't going to be at fault. Even if you're the world's best driver, some laws shift blame in unusual ways. Don't scrimp here.

Insurance Strategy No. 17: Determine Whether Your Rental Car Is Covered

This question comes up every time you rent a car and are offered the car company's insurance. In many cases, you are already covered, but find out *for sure*, once and for all, by reading your auto policy and discussing it with your agent.

If you are covered in a rental car by your policy, you probably will still be required to pay a deductible if you have an accident. If you discover that this is the case with your policy, then consider renting a car with a credit card that specifically covers the deductible as well. Check with American Express or MasterCard to get the right card with the right coverage. Be advised, however, that you're likely to spend a lot of time sorting out the insurance aftermath of a rental-car accident, with everyone trying to get everyone else to settle the claim. If you're traveling on business and the rental-car costs are reimbursable by the client, consider taking the coverage that the rental-car company offers. If you are traveling overseas, we also suggest you consider the rental-car company's insurance just to avoid the hassle of dealing with stateside coverage in a foreign country.

Insurance Strategy No. 18: Avoid Insurance Rip-Offs by Understanding the Best Values

As the preceding sections illustrate, we believe strongly in insurance. At the same time, we know it can get very expensive—and if you aren't careful, and aren't dealing with reputable people, you will get ripped off. So look out for yourself. Here are some ways to cut your costs:

★ *Increase your auto and homeowner's policies' deductibles to $500, or even $1,000.* Setting a very low deductible (such as $100) is simply too expensive. Check with your insurance company on the difference in the amount you pay for a policy with a $250, $500, and $1,000 deductible. The difference in what you'll pay is amazing. So raise your deductible to the highest level you're comfortable with.

★ *Reduce or get rid of life insurance on minor children.* The main purpose of life insurance is to protect dependents if the breadwinner dies. Minors normally do not contribute income that needs to be insured against loss. While the loss of a minor is a tragedy, there is usually no compelling reason to pay for life insurance on a child.

One exception to this rule is in the area of insurability. The insurance company may guarantee that the minor will always be insurable if you get coverage now. In that case, the key to consider is the amount of coverage. The company probably won't guarantee coverage for more than a small amount, so even here it may not be worth the cost.

★ *Consider last-to-die policies.* Last-to-die policies cover two people under one policy. They are traditionally cheaper than two policies on separate individuals, because the life expectancy tables based on the life of husband *and* wife favor the insurance company.

If you're using the insurance to protect you from taxes that may be paid on an estate, this is an excellent way to reduce your premiums and get maximum coverage. Another way to take advantage of a last-to-die policy is if either spouse has a health problem that makes individual insurance difficult to secure. Again, using last-to-die mortality tables helps spread the risk of coverage for the insurance companies, and so they are less restrictive on whom they cover.

YOUR MISSION TO WEALTH TO-DO LIST

1. **CONDUCT A PERSONAL INSURANCE AUDIT.** Review all your insurance policies to make sure that the plans you have are still adequate coverage for your current finances. Has your spouse started bringing in substantial money since you set up your policies? Could you live without that income? If not, your coverage isn't adequate.

2. **THINK HEALTH, LIFE, HOME, AND AUTO.** There are all kinds of insurance out there, but these are the Big Four. By now, you know that we never advocate buying anything you don't need. But insuring your health, life, home, and car are areas where we *never* scrimp. Comparison shop, yes; scrimp, no. Find the cheapest policy that meets all your needs. If you're rich, or *look* rich, buy more liability coverage.

3. **KEEP AN EYE ON DISABILITY AND LTC INSURANCE.** Disability insurance and long-term care insurance are two more kinds of insurance that you need to understand, comparison-shop for, and (probably) buy eventually. Remember, having a family changes everything.

4. **THINK DISCOUNTS AND BIG DEDUCTIBLES.** Having told you not to cut corners, now we'll tell you not to pay a nickel more than you have to. Find out if you qualify for any discounts. Figure out how much you can afford to pay at the front end of a given claim ($500? $1,000?), and use that as your deductible.

5. **DON'T LET YOUR COVERAGES LAPSE.** Make sure your new insurance is in place before you cancel your old policy. If you're leaving a job and you have no new health insurance in sight, sign up for COBRA coverage *before* you walk out that door.

★ ★ ★

CHAPTER 15

Make Your Life Less Taxing

Taxes, after all, are the dues that we pay for the privileges of membership in an organized society.

—Franklin Delano Roosevelt

More than a century ago, Mark Twain wrote that the difference between a taxidermist and a tax collector is that the taxidermist "takes only your skin." As we travel the country and speak with people who are in search of financial freedom, invariably the discussions turn to taxes. Yes, the tax code is always changing, and you have to keep your eye on it. But the truth is that in one form or another, taxes will always be with us. And as President Roosevelt said, taxes are really the fees that we should be prepared to pay for the privilege of living in an organized society.

That being said, you absolutely have to understand your tax obligations—and, specifically, what you can and cannot do to reduce those obligations.

We do *not* believe in, or promote, tax-dodging schemes. Instead, we are strong proponents of understanding what you can do legally, within the tax laws—and there is plenty. Most such tax savings involve the use of business structures, investments, trusts (see Chapter 16, "Build Your Family Financial Legacy"), or charities for which the government allows deductions. Understanding these rules, and using them to your advantage, is both important and responsible.

HOW MUCH TAX DO YOU PAY?

It is critically important for anyone who is seeking to come up with a productive tax reduction strategy to know his or her tax bracket. There are two categories of tax bracket that are most relevant to you: *effective* and *marginal*. Your effective tax bracket represents the percentage of your total income that you pay in taxes. For example, if you earned $50,000 last year and had to pay $8,000 in taxes, your effective tax bracket for last year was 16 percent ($8,000 divided by $50,000).

Your marginal tax rate is the percentage of your income that you pay in taxes on your highest dollar of earnings. Remember that our income tax system is *graduated* (rich people pay a higher percentage), and so the marginal tax rate increases as you earn more money.

When someone says that he is "in the 30 percent tax bracket," for example, he is telling you what he is paying on his top dollar of earnings, *not* that he is paying 30 percent of his total income in taxes. You need to know both your effective and your marginal tax brackets, so that you can gain a clearer picture of just where you stand.

Tax Strategy No. 1: Know Your Marginal Rate and the Value of a Deduction

Let's look at a simple example. If John Smith is single and earns $30,000 in 2005, we can see by looking at the tax rate schedules that he pays 10 percent in taxes on his first $6,000 in earnings ($600), 15 percent on the next $22,400 ($3,360), and 27 percent on the last $1,600 ($432). His marginal tax rate, then, is 27 percent, as that's the graduated rate that corresponds to his total income level. His effective rate (his total tax as a percentage of total income), however, is 14.64 percent ($4,392 divided by $30,000).

Knowing the breakdown of your effective tax rate in terms of the marginal tax rates you pay on your income will let you see on what part of your income you are paying the most to the taxing authorities. Gauging your earnings against the marginal tax rates will let you see when you are close to the next bracket, which in turn should motivate you to find more deductions or otherwise defer more income.

In our example, it would make sense for Smith to actively seek as many deductions as possible, and to become as aggressive as possible with his tax planning, as his expected future earnings creep higher and higher into the 27 percent range. While you should always endeavor to keep your tax burden as low as possible, keeping abreast of tax rate schedules will let you know when it becomes of particular importance, and will motivate you to find additional deductions.

As we touched on briefly, *brackets* are the tax percentages applied to each dollar earned within a range. Your taxable income (earnings after allowable deductions) determines which tax bracket you fall into. Here are the new federal brackets for personal earnings in 2005:

* *10 percent bracket.* Up to $7,300 for singles, $14,600 for couples filing jointly

* *15 percent bracket.* Up to $29,700 for singles and $59,400 for couples filing jointly

* *25 percent bracket.* Up to $71,950 for singles and up to $119,950 for couples filing jointly

* *28 percent bracket.* Up to $150,150 for singles and $182,800 for couples filing jointly

* *33 percent bracket.* Tops at $326,450 for both singles and couples filing jointly

* *35 percent bracket.* Applies to all income beyond $326,450

Tax Strategy No. 2: Use the Long Form When Filing Your Return

People often make the mistake of deciding that the amount of time they spend preparing their tax returns each year is more important than saving money. Because so many of us just want to get our taxes done and out of the way, we often miss out on money-saving deductions. But by so doing, we give away money.

One of the best examples is the decision to file using the short form, as opposed to the 1040 long form.

The government introduced the short forms (1040A and 1040EZ) some years ago, supposedly as a way of making life easier for taxpayers who fit a certain profile—usually some combination of particular marital status, income, and a few other criteria. We are not convinced; we think it's possible that the *real* reason for the creation of these short forms was that they might cut down on the number of deductions claimed each year, and Uncle Sam would reap more tax revenues.

If you file your return using a short form, you are *paying the maximum amount you can on that level of income,* because of the loss of potential deductions. When you file your return using the 1040 long form, by contrast, you can take all of the deductions that are available to you.

What normally happens with first-time long-form filers is that they learn about many deductions that they can't take advantage of. For

It is never wise to slip the hands of discipline.
—Lew Wallace

example, they haven't started a home-based business, or anything similar. No problem. The first time you fill out the long form, use it as an opportunity to see where your tax planning has been lacking. You will never pay more in taxes by using the long form, and once you become well versed in the available deductions by using the long form, you will always pay less—and probably a *lot* less.

Tax Strategy No. 3: Choose a Tax Preparer Who's Taxpayer Proactive

Tax preparation is big business. As each year begins, we are subjected to an onslaught of television, radio, and print ads for nationally recognized tax preparation services, as well as newspaper ads from local preparers. One national firm even offers a lottery as an incentive to get you in the door with your W-2s and receipts.

Having someone else prepare your taxes eliminates virtually all of the hassle and strain that goes along with the annual filing process. That can be a nice benefit, but it is *not* the reason you should hire a preparer. If you are going to pay someone else to do your taxes, then you should do so because you are confident that he or she can save you *significantly more money* than you could on your own.

We have found that there are basically two kinds of tax preparers: those who do taxes simply to get them done, and those who try to save you as much as they can. Believe it or not, true tax preparation professionals *like* doing tax returns. They view each return as a challenge: to see just how much they can save you in taxes. These are the only preparers you should use.

> *Don't be afraid to challenge the pros, even in their own backyard.*
>
> —Colin Powell

You want to be especially wary of tax preparers who seem quick to advise you against claiming a deduction because it might make you a good candidate for an audit. As long as you have the appropriate backup for any deductions you wish to claim, your tax preparer should claim them.

In fact, a good preparer will take it upon him- or herself, while completing your tax return, to ask you about possible opportunities to claim deductions you haven't considered. The tax preparer's whole effort on your behalf should be to help you find additional, legitimate tax savings. In short, your tax preparer should be taxpayer-proactive.

Tax Strategy No. 4: Deduct It If You Believe It

Many people are afraid to claim certain deductions because they feel that doing so will raise a "red flag" with the IRS. Don't worry about that. As long as you can provide a reasonable explanation as to why you should be entitled to a certain deduction, then take it. If the IRS has a question about it, simply be prepared to offer your justification. If you are too timid about claiming deductions, you will end up paying more taxes than you should.

Most people fail to claim all the deductions they are entitled to. Don't be one of them. Claim all of the legitimate deductions you can, and you will find that the amount of money you save is well worth running the risk of questions from the IRS. Just keep backup information on the deduction you claim.

Tax Strategy No. 5: Keep Note of the Most Overlooked Deductions

The IRS keeps track of the deductions that are most frequently overlooked by taxpayers. If you are new to the world of tax reduction, then it may well be that you are completely unfamiliar with the numerous deduction opportunities that exist.

Following is a list of the deductions that are most frequently overlooked by taxpayers. Mind you, this is not a list of all available deductions, as that list would be a book in itself. These are just the deductions that the greatest number of eligible people fail to take. As you go through the list, make a note of each deduction that you feel may apply to you.

Please note that there are exceptions and special qualifications for many of these, so you must review the details of each to know if and how you may qualify to take them. The instruction booklet that accompanies your Form 1040 sent each year by Uncle Sam will be of great assistance in this regard.

Deductions Related to Health Care
* Treatment for alcoholism and drug addiction
* Contact lenses

* Prescription contraceptives
* Premiums for health insurance
* Hearing aids
* Hospital services
* Medical transportation
* Orthopedic shoes
* Seeing-eye dogs
* Physician-prescribed diet foods
* Equipment used by the disabled
* Specialized schools for handicapped children

Deductions Related to Employment

* Work tools with a life of one year or less
* Moving expenses associated with a job-related move
* Real estate sales commissions associated with a sale of your home that is job-related
* Labor union dues
* Costs of an education to maintain/improve job skills
* Fees paid to employment agencies
* Résumé preparation costs if the new job is in your present career field
* Cost of uniforms
* 50 percent of self-employment tax

Deductions Related to Investment Expenses

* Custodial fees paid for IRAs and other tax-deferred retirement accounts (if paid separately and outside of the monies in the account itself)
* Cost of investment magazines and newspapers
* Fees paid for tax/investment advice

★ 50 percent of the cost of entertainment (including meals) when meeting with tax/investment advisors

★ Cost of safe deposit box(es)

Deductions Related to Mortgage Interest

★ Interest paid on a first or second home

★ Second mortgage/home equity loan interest

★ Interest on an RV and/or boat if it is used as a second home and has a kitchen, bath, and sleeping quarters

Miscellaneous Deductions

★ Tax preparation fees

★ Casualty and theft loses

★ Foreign taxes

★ Gambling losses (up to the total of winnings)

★ Penalties for mortgage prepayment

★ Penalties incurred by early withdrawals of savings

★ Points paid on an original mortgage

★ State personal property taxes on cars

Again, there are various limitations on the deductions on this list, and we encourage you to order the IRS's free publication to get specifics on your situation.

Tax Strategy No. 6: Never Apply Your Refund to the Following Year's Taxes

When you complete your tax return using Form 1040, you will notice an option located at the end of the document to have your refund *not* sent to you directly, but instead applied to the following year's taxes (this, of course, assumes that you are receiving a refund).

While such an idea might make sense at first glance, do *not* take the IRS up on its convenient offer. While it is easy to see why you might want to check that box—after all, you're going to have to pay taxes in some amount next year, anyway—the reality is that when you select this option, you're letting the IRS use your money for free.

Take your refund and deposit it into your investment account. Now, instead of giving free money to the IRS, you're using your own money to make even more money for yourself.

Tax Strategy No. 7: Eliminate Your Refunds Forever

As long as we are on the topic of refunds, we think you should try to eliminate them altogether. "What?" you may be asking. "Give up that spring bonus?"

Yes. If you are getting a refund, you have spent the past calendar year making a tax-free loan to Uncle Sam. Yes, it was a forced savings tool—but at zero interest paid, it was pretty expensive. If you are getting a refund every year, you are having too much taken out of your paycheck in withholdings. Reduce the withholdings and increase the net you get each month.

> *I don't believe in principle, but I do in interest.*
> —James Russell Lowell

One question that we hear asked a lot by taxpayers who are due a refund is, "When should I expect my refund check?" Most people don't have any idea that the IRS is *required* to send you your refund check within 45 days of the date you file (or April 15, whichever is later). If your refund is late, then guess what? The IRS has to pay *you* interest.

Don't be lazy about this. Count the days from the day you file your return. If you receive your refund check more than 45 days later, contact the IRS, and ask how to submit a claim for interest on the number of extra days it took your refund to arrive.

Tax Strategy No. 8: File Your Return as Late as Possible

One of the simplest, but most effective, strategies you can use to minimize your chances of being selected for an audit involves nothing more than the decision about when to file your return. Did you know that you can greatly reduce the likelihood of being selected for an audit simply by mailing your return as late as possible? It isn't a terribly sophisticated strategy. But it works.

The reason returns that are filed later have less chance of being audited is because of the way returns are selected for audit by the IRS's computers. Basically, the IRS tells the computer to select a certain number of returns for audit from each category of deduction available. Once the computer has selected the quota-based number of returns per category, it stops selecting. Even if you have actually completed your tax return early, you may want to get an automatic two-month extension to file late. Wait to mail it until as late as possible. Filing extensions does not eliminate your requirement that you have all of your taxes in by April 15. If you pay the tax later when you file or if you owe more than you calculated, you will pay interest on the amount due and late payment penalties.

You can also seek an extension to as late as October 15 to actually file your return, but you have to get approval based on a legitimate business reason, such as inability to get all of your information in a timely manner.

Tax Strategy No. 9: Prepare for the Audit

If you are ever notified by the IRS that you will be subject to an audit of your tax return, you are likely to be a bit shaken. We're all familiar with the horror stories that describe how the lives of decent people have been ruined by an out-of-control audit. Nevertheless, if you are notified that you will be audited, you must get past this initial reaction as quickly as possible, and focus on preparing for the audit.

After you've received notice of an impending audit, the first step is to look closely at the audit notice, and see if it fully informs you as to the following three issues:

★ The reason you are being audited
★ The part(s) of your return that will be audited
★ The documentation that the IRS specifically wants to review

The IRS must provide this information to you, in writing, before it can demand that you appear for your audit. While the notice you receive from the IRS informing you of the audit will contain some of this information, be firm and ask for more specificity when you contact the agency.

For example, although the notice will provide a "reason" why you are being audited, do not be shy about having your tax preparer inquire as to why the IRS believes you owe more taxes, and what part(s) of the return will be audited. If it is unclear, contact the IRS to find out. *The audit can cover only those parts of your return that the IRS states in writing will be subject to review.* With regard to the matter of documentation, again, ask for specifics. Ask the IRS to list precisely what pieces of documentation it wants you to bring. Don't bring any more information to the audit than you may need to prove your point.

If you are audited and the audit requires an office visit, you should hire someone to go in your place. Just as you should hire an attorney if you have a legal problem, you should take an audit seriously enough to send someone else in your place. It is much easier for a professional to argue with the IRS than it is for you to do that.

It is important when you haven't got any ammunition to have a butt on your rifle.

—Winston Churchill

First, tax professionals understand the procedures, and may even know the auditor personally. In addition, your representative can argue your points with the agent, whereas if you argue, the agent might take it personally and get more aggressive. It just makes sense to get an experienced pro on your side.

YOUR HOME BUSINESS— THE LAST GREAT TAX SHELTER

We address this issue in our business strategies section (see Chapter 17), but it is so important that it is also worth mentioning here. There are few tax shelters that are better than a small, home-based business. In addition, there are other things that your home can offer for tax deductions. Read on.

Tax Strategy No. 10: Start a Home-Based Business

The reason a home-based business is such a terrific tax shelter is that the cost and expenses of anything and everything used in your business become deductible to the extent that they are used in that business. A great example of this is your car. Your car is a nondeductible expense when you use it as a family vehicle. Use it partially in your business, however, and it becomes a partial tax deduction.

Think of all the household goods and services you use in the course of a month. By using them in your home-based business, even part of the time, you can turn them into tax deductions.

While there are other great reasons for starting a small business in your home, the tax benefits of doing so are among the very best. Again, your primary goal in developing a sound tax reduction strategy is to get as many deductions for yourself as you possibly can. Not only do you want to make certain that you are taking all of the deductions to which you are currently entitled, but you should be aggressive in seeking ways you can become eligible for others. Think of these efforts as a part-time job in itself—one that may not give you a paycheck, but still will put thousands of dollars back into your pocket each year.

Tax Strategy No. 11: Earn Deductions from Much of What You Already Own

Another place to find deductions is around your home, where you can find plenty of goods that you use little or even not at all. Rather than throwing them away, donate them to qualified charities.

It's likely that you have a lot of stuff around your home that's suitable for donation. You can deduct contributions you make in the form of cash, securities, real estate, and physical property to such charities. If you contribute at least $250 in any form to a charity, you must obtain a receipt from the charity. The receipts you receive normally will not indicate the value of what you donated. It is up to you to cite a figure, and you need to be as accurate as possible about the number.

Make sure you keep track of all your donations: clothes, shoes, books, furniture—even cars. All these things add up. When you combine those with any monetary donations, your total charitable contributions can lead to a hefty tax deduction.

> *What I gave, I have;*
> *what I spent, I had;*
> *what I kept, I lost.*
>
> —Old epitaph

Note that if you donate physical property to a charity for which you claim a value of $500 or greater, you must complete IRS Form 8283 and attach it to your 1040. If the value of what you donate is more than $5,000, then you must submit a written appraisal with your return.

Don't let yourself to be put off from making these donations simply because there is a little paperwork involved. Contributing the numerous goods and other things that you no longer need to charity can be a large source of deductions for you, and end up saving you a bunch of money at tax time. And, of course, it's an opportunity for you to help those who are less fortunate than yourself, by giving them access to things that they can put to better use than you can.

YOUR MISSION TO WEALTH TO-DO LIST

1. FIGURE OUT WHERE YOU ARE NOW. Determine your personal effective and marginal tax rates, so that you will have a sense of where the tax-bracket breakpoints

are. As you approach a higher tax bracket (we assume), you'll be more motivated to seek out those extra legitimate deductions.

2. YOU'RE ONLY DOING WHAT'S LEGAL AND FAIR. One of the first things you have to lodge firmly in your head is that minimizing your taxes in every legitimate way that is open to you is both legal and fair. Even the IRS doesn't expect you to pay more than you're required to pay. Don't.

3. THINK "LONG FORM" AND "ACTIVIST PROFESSIONALS." Start using the IRS's long form, so that you can get a feel for where you can find extra legitimate deductions. If you use a professional tax preparer, make sure that he or she is not simply punching the clock, but is determined to find every possible legitimate deduction.

4. DON'T LEND THE FEDS MONEY. You need it more than they do. Take your refund (don't apply it to next year's taxes), and put it in your investment account. If you find that you're getting refunds every year, it means you're having too much withheld, and you are loaning the Feds money all year long. Don't.

5. BE AUDIT-SAVVY. File late (within the IRS's guidelines) to minimize your chances of being audited. If you *do* get audited, don't panic. Working with your tax preparer (if you use one), get the IRS to clearly define the limits of the audit. Then go in with your receipts and your

self-confidence—or, better yet, send that tax preparer. You haven't done anything wrong; you now have to demonstrate that to the IRS.

6. USE YOUR HOME TO SHELTER MORE INCOME. A home-based business is one of the best (legitimate) tax shelters around. Read Chapter 17 to learn more. Also, look around your home for anything that you can give away and take a charitable deduction on. You'll help people in need, and also help yourself.

★ ★ ★

CHAPTER 16

Build Your Family Financial Legacy

All of the links in the chain pulled together,
and the chain became unbreakable.

—George S. Patton

Even after you achieve your goal of financial freedom, your journey isn't over. Your next two challenges will be to hang on to your money and to learn how to use it to help your family and others.

For some people, holding on to their money is harder than making it in the first place. It becomes a psychological burden. Even if they aren't actually experiencing any difficulty, they begin to worry constantly about their money, and whether they will have enough to last out their years. Even the super-rich are not immune to this phobia. They imagine illnesses that might befall them, burning up all their wealth. They are no longer financially free.

Truly successful people understand how they gained their financial freedom. They have acquired self-confidence from that process, and they understand that they are surrounded by abundance. Money in the bank is only one small part of that abundance. They understand that whatever resources they need, they will be able to obtain. These people view their millionaire status with a confidence derived from experience. They are determined to instill this same kind of confidence in their children.

I am lord of myself, accountable to none.

—Benjamin Franklin

One example is Warren Buffett. Generally acknowledged to be the wealthiest person in the United States, Buffett has publicly stated that he will leave most of his wealth to charity, rather than to his children. Why? Because he believes that inherited wealth takes away from a person's ability to develop self-confidence. The truth is, you have to *make it on your own*. Buffett didn't want his children to miss out on that opportunity. Instead of cash, he is leaving his children a much more valuable legacy: self-confidence.

Financial Legacy Strategy No. 1: Pass On What You Have Learned

There is an old saying which is one of our favorites: "Give a man a fish, and you feed him for a day; teach him to fish, and you feed him for a lifetime." That quote captures the main point of this chapter. Once you have mastered the principles of this book, you need to pass them on. You need to teach others to fish.

Your children are a good place to start—but don't stop there. There are many people around you who are eager to learn what you have learned. Not only will *they* profit from sharing your experience; so will you. You will experience the joy and pleasure that comes from giving.

Our progress as a nation can be no swifter than our progress in education.

—John Fitzgerald Kennedy

We Americans today are very lucky. Because of advances in science and medicine, we are living longer and staying healthier longer. In previous generations, age 65 was *old*. When people got to that age, they retired, hoping to live a few more years to enjoy the fruits of their labor. Today, 65 is just another birthday, from a physical standpoint.

But some people still look forward to 65 as a watershed event— as the *end* of something. One reason is that these people are unhappy with their jobs or with some other aspect of their lives. They mistakenly believe that because of their retirement, things will change. They won't. If these people want to move on with their lives, they should move on *now*. If they want to do a different kind of work, they should make that change *now*.

No, we're not suggesting that you give up on your responsibilities, head off to the mountains, and meditate on the meaning of life. What we are saying is that the strategies in this book give you the knowledge and tools to make *any change you want* in your life, and to do it sooner rather than later. There will be some interim sacrifices. But if the change is something you want, it's worth it.

How are you going to live the rest of your life? What legacy do you want to leave? How can you protect what you have now, and what you will have in the future? These are key questions. Answering them will take thought, planning, and continual updating. In the next few pages, we want to give you additional ideas to think about, and take action on.

Financial Legacy Strategy No. 2: Plan Your Death to Make Your Life Meaningful

We are always amazed at the people who plan their lives to the last detail, but don't spend any time at all on their deaths. It is as though they feel they can somehow avoid the inevitable by ignoring it. In fact, you owe it to yourself and your heirs to make plans for your death. Naturally, there are some serious and important things to plan for, but you should also do some things for fun. Here are some ideas:

* *Fund a $1,000 scholarship at your high school.* Do you know how important a $1,000 scholarship is to some kids? Not only does it help the child financially, but it helps her or him emotionally as a powerful confidence builder. You can fund such a scholarship in perpetuity with a $10,000 gift that earns 10 percent income. Fund the scholarship while you are still alive, and go back to your high school every year to give out the award. You'll have a blast.

* *Donate a park.* Wouldn't it be nice to have your own small park for kids to enjoy? Perhaps the cost of such a commitment is too much for you. How about a fountain, a playground, or any number of specific things that you can give for the lasting happiness of others? Remember, even a book donated by you to your public library is something that has lasting value.

* *Adopt a child.* Share your life. Even if you can't adopt, get involved with youth organizations. One organization that we have worked with meets in people's homes, and helps teens to grow personally and spiritually. It is a joy

for us to be a part of this group and to have a succession of wonderful young people fill our house with smiles and song. Find an organization in your community that deals with kids, and offer your physical and financial help.

Financial Legacy Strategy No. 3: Protect Your Family by Writing a Will

Everyone needs a will. It doesn't matter where you live or how much money you have; you need a will. Even if you have a living trust, as we discuss later, you will need a will to deal with your other assets.

If you have minor children, a will is especially important, because you need to designate a guardian for your children. *This is critically important.* Without a will, if you and your spouse both died at the same time, the state court system would decide your children's fate (where they would wind up), and this is *not* something that you want to have happen. Find someone whom you trust and who is willing to take on guardianship responsibility, and put that in your will. Then leave the will in a place where it can be found. (Your attorney is one possibility; a safe deposit box is another.)

If you don't have a will, you can go into any good bookstore and buy a form that applies to your state. A good will package is published by NOLO Legal Publishers and Quicken, the accounting software company. The software and book are called Quicken Willmaker Plus. Try it; you'll be surprised how easy it is.

> *One minute you're a hawk in the skies, the next you are an ant on the ground.*
>
> —Unknown soldier, Persian Gulf war

Financial Legacy Strategy No. 4: Create a Living Will

What do you want to have happen if you are incapacitated and can't make medical decisions for yourself? The answer to this question is very important, and it may be different from your spouse's view and that of other members of your family. Failure to make provision for cessation of artificial life support in such circumstances (should that be your desire) can result in a large financial burden for your family by having your assets depleted for medical expenses not covered by insurance and/or by making it impossible for your heirs to inherit in a timely fashion.

To make sure that your wishes are followed, get a medical authorization form approved for your state and fill it out. (The Quicken Willmaker Plus program also contains this information.) This form, along with your living will, defines the type of medical care you want in specific circumstances and designates someone to make those decisions. Obviously, you need to appoint someone who agrees with you about the use of life-support systems, "heroic" medical steps to prolong life, and so on. Talk all this through. Consider asking your attorney to draft a thorough, personalized statement of your intent. Have that statement witnessed and notarized.

Living Wills and Medical Directives Protect Your Life Care

Read carefully and make sure you understand any legal form that you sign. We have seen forms designated by hospitals as "Standard Living Wills and Medical Authorizations." Upon reading these forms, we were shocked to discover that they give the hospital and doctors the absolute authority to withhold any life-saving equipment, including a ventilator.

This form gives too much power to someone outside your inner circle. There are many reasons a person might go on a ventilator. For instance, anyone with major respiratory problems would die without it. With one, you may fully recover. Please make sure that any form you sign makes clear the condition you must be in before such equipment can be shut off or denied to you. We would also suggest you write on a card where the form and your living will are located, and carry that card in your wallet.

Give Part of Yourself to Someone Else

What are you going to do with your organs when you die? Don't waste them. Live on in another person.

Sign an organ donor card, and carry it in your wallet. In some cases, the hospital has only a few hours to make critical decisions on organ use. Having the card on your person could give them that time. If you don't know where to get a donor card, start with your local hospital as a point of contact.

THE LONG-TERM POWERS OF TRUSTS

The most common misunderstanding about trusts is the idea that they are just for wealthy people. This arises from the belief that the primary reason for having a trust is to save on estate taxes, and therefore if you don't have a big estate, you're OK without a trust. This is a *big mistake*. Even people with modest assets benefit from putting a trust in place.

Expense is another reason we hear for not setting up a trust. Even if you go to a high-powered attorney and have a trust set up for you and your spouse with additional wills, it shouldn't cost you more than $1,500. There are other options, ranging from $25 do-it-yourself kits to $500 vehicles set up by trust companies, but this is another one of those areas where we don't recommend scrimping. Yes, this is money you'll have to pay now (as opposed to probate costs, which your heirs will have to pay). But if you really feel strongly about this, ask your heirs to put up the $1,500 for you. We can guarantee that this will be the fastest money you have ever raised.

Another excuse that we've frequently heard for not setting up a trust is that the couple holds everything in joint ownership, with right of survivorship, and therefore doesn't need a trust. At best (and we stress "at best"), joint ownership will defer probate on a particular piece of property only until the last of the two individuals dies. And in fact, joint ownership can create problems, because property can't be conveyed without all parties' signatures. If a problem develops between the joint owners, it may take a court intervention to resolve it.

Perhaps the biggest reason people don't set up a trust is that they fear losing control. But this fear is *absolutely, totally* unfounded if you go the route of a *revocable living trust.* You are the party in control. In fact, you can be all of the parties in the trust: the grantor (the person who sets up the trust), the beneficiary (the person who gets the benefits of the trust), and the trustee (the person who runs the trust).

The battle, sir, is not to the strong alone; it is to the vigilant, the active, the brave.

—Patrick Henry

You are probably wondering how you can be the *beneficiary* of a trust. (Don't you have to die first?) The fact is that you can be the beneficiary while you are alive, and receive income and other benefits from the trust. There are other beneficiaries, named by you, who step forward after your death. The point is that while you are alive, *you have control.* You can change your mind at any time.

Tax Strategy No. 5: Use Trusts to Avoid Probate and Save on Estate Taxes

By now, you know the benefits of simply setting up a trust: no probate, disability protection, child protection, time, and other costs. As we also mentioned, another benefit is saving on estate taxes. The amount you save on these taxes will depend upon how much you have. Remember, for many people, this isn't *the* reason to have a trust, but for others, it is a big benefit.

Estate taxes aren't complicated; they are just *expensive*, and they follow the government's schedule. Estate taxes must be paid within nine months of death, and they must be paid in cash. The government will not care that the estate is tied up in probate because of the lack of a valid will. It won't care that the real estate market is soft, or that stocks are temporarily down. It will demand its money—in cash, now. If everything must be sold at auction, so be it. Harsh, but true.

Your objective in using a trust is to reduce taxes as much as possible. In addition, you may want to use life insurance to help fund a separate life insurance trust, and distribute the proceeds in such a way that they won't be taxable at all. Interested? Read on.

Our tax system provides for a graduated estate tax based on assets. (Yes, there is a lot of talk about a permanent repeal of the estate tax, but until that happens, you need to make plans.) For 2005, the first $1.5 million is exempt (see the table that follows).

In addition, there is an unlimited marital deduction. This means that the government will defer tax on a couple's estate until the death of the second spouse. Then the government collects on what remains of the combined assets of the couple. Consequently, from a federal standpoint, if the value of the combined estate is below $3 million and you use the trust to plan properly, no federal estate taxes will be due (although there may be state estate taxes or inheritance taxes due).

An important point to consider is that an estate is frequently worth more than people think. The estate taxes are calculated on *everything*, including the current value of your home and property, retirement plans, and any life insurance you may have that is not separated in a different trust. Upon the death of the first spouse, the marital deduction eliminates tax. However, upon the death of the second spouse, both their assets are combined, and the estate still gets an exemption of only $1.5 million.

A revocable living trust can be used to separate the assets of the married couple, creating what is called an "A/B Trust" or a "his and hers" trust. This establishes the trust as having two parts. Upon the death of the first spouse, the assets of that spouse will go to the named beneficiary, who is *someone other than the surviving spouse*. The beneficiary is normally a child (or children) of the couple.

The children don't get to do anything with the assets yet, because the surviving spouse gets the benefit of those assets for life, to be used for his or her health, education, or welfare. Upon the death of the second spouse, the remaining assets can be distributed. The result of using the trust is that instead of sheltering $1.5 million from estate taxes, you have sheltered $3 million. How much money did this save? A 47 percent tax on $1.5 million, plus any state taxes, probate costs, and attorney's fees.

Is it worth shelling out $1,500 to have an attorney set this plan up? Absolutely.

THE PERSONAL ESTATE TAX EXEMPTION

YEAR	ESTATE TAX EXEMPTION	HIGHEST ESTATE AND GIFT TAX RATE
2002	$1 million	50%
2003	$1 million	49%
2004	$1.5 million	48%
2005	$1.5 million	47%
2006	$2 million	46%
2007	$2 million	45%
2008	$2 million	45%
2009	$3.5 million	45%
2010	Estate tax repealed	Top individual income tax rate (gift tax only)
2011	$1 million unless Congress extends repeal	55% unless Congress extends repeal

Tax Strategy No. 6: Use an Irrevocable Life Insurance Trust to Build an Estate Tax-Free

As noted earlier, when an individual dies, all of that individual's assets are included in his or her estate. This means that a life insurance policy purchased to help pay estate taxes is also included, and would take the estate into a higher tax bracket.

The way to avoid this added cost is to purchase the life insurance policy, but make an insurance trust, rather than an individual, the beneficiary. The result is that *none* of the insurance proceeds are included in the estate.

How much does this trust save? In our previous example of the $3 million estate, all additional proceeds would be taxed at 47 percent. If the deceased had a $500,000 life insurance policy outside of the trust, using the life insurance trust would save $235,000 in taxes.

Tax Strategy No. 7: Don't Forget to Fund the Trust

Let's assume that you are motivated enough by this information to set up a trust for yourself and your family. If you do, please remember this one very important point: you *must* fund (transfer assets to) the trust. This means that you must retitle all of your holdings in the name of the trust. This is the biggest hassle you will face in establishing your trust, but it must be done. Bank accounts, real estate, securities: Everything must now be held in the name of the trust. But this is not as burdensome as it may seem, because title companies, brokerage firms, and banks are prepared to handle it for you.

The other thing to remember about funding your trust is that once it is established, all new purchases or investments should also be put in the name of the trust. Again, no big deal. You just have to remember to do it. If you don't, then the assets are not trust assets, but belong to the named titleholder.

While the funding concept seems simple enough, time and time again, people forget to carry it out. All your efforts are wasted if you forget to retitle your assets in the name of the trust. You must fund a trust in order to take advantage of it.

Tax Strategy No. 8: Use Trusts in Retirement Plans to Save Even More Money

Chances are that most of you already *have* one type of trust. If you have a retirement plan such as an IRA, Keogh, 401(k),

403(b), or some other similar plan, you are using a form of trust.

These programs are designed to benefit the named holder of the plan. They cannot be retitled into your trust, nor can they be held jointly with another individual. However, upon the death of the plan owner, the proceeds of the retirement plan do escape probate, unless you have (1) named your estate as beneficiary or (2) failed to name anyone. Surprisingly, this does happen, particularly in the case of single individuals.

Retirement plans, as we all know, are tax-deferred. Simple life planning would teach us to utilize all methods of keeping these funds deferred as long as possible. Under normal rules, when an individual dies, the retirement plan's assets are paid out and all taxes are due. The one exception to this is if a spouse is the named beneficiary and the spouse elects to exercise a spousal rollover provision.

This option allows the spouse to roll over the retirement plan assets into his or her own IRA. Even if the spouse didn't have an IRA, the law allows him or her to set one up for this specific purpose. By using this option, taxes will continue to be deferred on the spouse's IRA. Because of this special provision, the spouse should be the primary beneficiary of *any* retirement plan.

But who should be the contingent beneficiary? Who should be the beneficiary if you have no spouse? These are important planning questions, because IRAs can be stretched to go on for years, and—during this continuous period—will continue to defer any current tax on the growth. The compounded growth on a stretched IRA can be a major asset builder for families.

> *A man is never so on trial as in the moment of excessive good fortune.*
>
> —Lew Wallace

IRREVOCABLE TRUSTS AND THEIR PROTECTIVE DEVICES

We are a litigious society. We don't need to tell you how often these days someone says, "Let's sue." Wishing it weren't so won't change the reality. The result of the litigation phenomenon is that anyone with assets is a target. Professional malpractice claims, business errors and omissions, car and property accidents are all potential hazards that could at any time deprive us and our family of everything we have worked so hard for. Certain types of trusts can protect you and your family from these hazards.

Liability protective trusts tend to be more complicated than normal revocable trusts and require special provisions. In most cases, to achieve asset protection, you will need to have an *irrevocable* trust, rather than a revocable trust. There are, of course, some disadvantages to this type of trust—primarily the control that you surrender.

Nevertheless, if you have a high-profile profession, giving up some control will be a lot less costly than giving up your assets in a lawsuit. In many cases, once opposing attorneys find that you are protected with trusts, the threatened lawsuits will simply go away.

Financial Legacy Strategy No. 9: Use Irrevocable Trusts for Asset Protection

If you believe that you are in need of this specialized form of financial planning, we encourage you to retain a lawyer who is expert in this area. Normally, this will be a trust and estate planning expert. You can either check your local Yellow Pages for that designation or call your local bar association for a list of attorneys with that specialty. A trusted friend's recommendation may be the best starting point.

Financial Legacy Strategy No. 10: Make a Will to Successfully Plan Life

After all of this talk about trusts, you may assume that we'll let you off the hook about that will. Unfortunately, that is not the case. Even though you have a trust, you will still need a will to handle loose ends. The type of will you will need with a trust is called a "pour-over." The term *pour-over* simply means that everything you have remaining outside your trust pours over into your trust at your death. This may be nothing, or it may be a lot.

The pour-over will is simply added protection in case you forgot to title something in the name of your trust, if it wasn't done right, or if you inherited something that didn't get placed inside the trust. Whatever the reason, it is your final protection to make sure your life ends the way you want it.

Financial Legacy Strategy No. 11: Use Corporations to Protect Your Personal Assets

You don't *have* to have a corporation to run your business out of, but we do recommend it. You can protect your personal assets by using a corporation to operate your business. If any business liability is created, it is limited to the assets of your business, and—unless you also guaranteed the liability personally—a creditor can't come after you personally.

Sole proprietorships and partnerships don't provide the same liability protection. They create unreasonable exposure for your personal assets for actions of both yourself and your partner, if you have one. Form a corporation for each business venture you start.

There are three different types of corporations that you can use: a C corporation, a subchapter S corporation, or an LLC (limited liability company). The subchapter S and the LLC have pass-through tax benefits that can be very attractive to the owners of small businesses. In other words, the corporation's profits and losses pass through directly to the shareholders. Structured correctly, you can shift gains and losses to yourself and other members of your family, depending on circumstances.

The C corporation form has its own advantages, including the ability to retain earnings in the corporation and to establish medical reimbursement plans for owners as employees. You should definitely check with an attorney about these organizational options.

Financial Legacy Strategy No. 12: Decrease Your Personal Liability

It isn't always easy to avoid personal liability, because all lenders want you to personally guarantee loans you take out with them. This means that all of your other assets are pledged, in addition to the one you are borrowing on. If you default on the loan, the lender can take the collateral or come after your other assets.

It is impossible to win the great prizes of life without running risks.

—Theodore Roosevelt

Sometimes you have no choice but to give a personal guarantee. You want your business to grow, so you take the risk. That's OK, if you understand the risk versus reward of what you are doing. But we have seen other situations where people sign personal guarantees that make no sense. A parent with a high net worth guarantees a loan for a child's business and has no understanding of the documents. The loan is increased and expanded over the years to grow the business. One day, a problem occurs, and the loan is called. The business goes under, and the parent is asked to make good on the loan guarantee he or she signed years before on a much smaller amount.

Never sign anything that exposes all of your assets unless you fully understand the ramifications of what you are signing. If you don't, get a lawyer. If you *must* co-sign a loan, try these three strategies:

1. Limit the personal liability to a certain time frame.
2. Limit the liability to a maximum amount.
3. Require the lender to collect from all assets and all other borrowers first.

In addition to your personal guarantee, lenders will frequently ask for your spouse's personal guarantee, to give them the chance to go after his or her assets as well. This is another negotiable point; don't give in on this one too easily.

Financial Legacy Strategy No. 13: Use Charitable Giving for Win-Win

As your assets grow, charitable trusts can be established that fund all your needs while you're alive, but pass those assets to your favorite charity upon your death. You can get immediate tax deductions for the gift, you can structure income for your life, and you can provide for your favorite charity after you are gone.

There are many tax advantages to these trusts, which are also beneficial to the receiving organization. The charitable trust can also be combined with the life insurance trust mentioned previously.

Proper combination of the two trusts allows you to pass the same amount to your heirs and provide charitable benefits as well—a true win-win situation for all. Ask your charity of choice for its materials on "planned gifts," a category that includes charitable lead trusts, charitable remainder trusts, bequests, and other vehicles. Then consult your lawyer and your financial planner.

Financial Legacy Strategy No. 14: Define the Economics of Marriage

Discussions about prenuptial and postnuptial agreements are usually not pleasant, because they require the participants to think about scenarios in which the marriage doesn't work out. The fact is, however, that half of all marriages fail. So thinking about the "economics of marriage" is only practical.

Prenuptial agreements have been used by the wealthy for years, mainly to handle the situation of a poor person marrying into a rich family. They define what happens financially in case of a divorce. If you or your spouse has been married before, they are also a helpful tool to make special financial arrangements for children of previous marriages.

Postnuptial agreements are growing in popularity. Wayward spouses are being forced to sign these agreements as a condition of being allowed back into the relationship. They are definitely enforceable, although someone is certain to argue that they were signed under duress.

While we normally believe in and encourage self-law, do not try

Never become so consumed by your career that nothing is left that belongs only to you and your family.

—Colin Powell

to draft these agreements yourself. Courts almost always require both parties to have had a separate attorney, in order for them to be enforceable.

Financial Legacy Strategy No. 15: Build the Family Fortress

As you grow more comfortable with your money, you should consider forming family limited partnerships to run your joint businesses and investments. A limited partnership is a specific legal entity, comprising one or more general partners and one or more limited partners. The general partners have control and liability; limited partners have no control but also no liability. If you use a limited partnership, you can be the general partner and maintain total control over the assets. The other participating members of your family will be limited partners.

Structuring limited partnerships with family members allows you to shift ownership interests in your assets while still maintaining control. Shifting the assets earlier decreases the value of your estate, and consequently the potential taxes. During your life, you can also reduce income taxes by structuring the partnership so that more income goes to your children. This generally makes sense, because your children are normally in a lower tax bracket than you and your spouse.

The limited partnership is also an ideal tool to use in family business affairs, because it limits liability for participants (except the general partner), yet allows you to structure financial arrangements that benefit individual family members differently.

You can also limit the general partner's liability by forming a corporation that is 100 percent owned by the senior family member. The corporation's general partner avoids individual liability, but is still able to run the affairs of the family limited partnership because she or he is the owner of the company.

In all of these cases, read up on the structure, get a sense of how it might work for you, and then consult your attorney. Make sure your attorney is experienced enough in these specialized realms to really help you.

YOUR MISSION TO WEALTH TO-DO LIST

1. **PASS ON WHAT YOU KNOW, NOT WHAT YOU OWN.** While you certainly want to provide for your family, make sure you don't bury their initiative and self-esteem in wealth. Teach them "how to fish."

2. **MAKE YOUR LIFE MEANINGFUL.** Think about your legacy. What do you want to be remembered for? What gives you joy? How can you bring those things together in your life (and make them your legacy, as well)?

3. **WILLS AND LIVING WILLS SPEAK FOR YOU WHEN YOU CAN'T.** Set up your affairs so that you're not at the whim of a hospital, and so that your children aren't at the whim of a probate court judge. Write your will, and keep it up to date.

4. **EXPLORE HOW TRUSTS CAN WORK FOR YOU.** Trusts aren't just for rich people anymore. In fact, they are an essential tool in estate planning, even if you're

not Rockefeller-rich. The right trust (including an irrevocable life insurance trust) can reduce your estate tax enormously.

5. **BUILD YOUR FAMILY FORTRESS.** In every legal and financial move you make, look for opportunities to include competent and interested family members in either active or passive roles. You will gain flexibility, control your liability, minimize your taxes—and maybe get some excellent talent into the business.

★ ★ ★

CHAPTER 17

Build Your Own Business

He who has his thumb on the purse has the power.

—Otto von Bismarck

Financial freedom comes in many forms, and we would be remiss if we didn't discuss the value of building a family-run business. This isn't for everybody, of course. Some readers may find the idea of having their own business exciting; others may consider it the last thing in the world they want to do. You make the call—but at least try the idea on for size.

For us, entrepreneurship is a way of life.

It seems that we have been involved with building businesses since we were teenagers. We have created many businesses over the years, and these businesses have created great opportunities for many members of the family. In our current financial services and software business, we have five family members working together on various assignments. While we don't always agree, we always respect one another's opinions and ideas. Even when we disagree, we always find a way to do it respectfully, and we make sure that the matter is resolved with no hard feelings.

Having a family business does *not* mean that you all have to work together in close quarters. It simply means that you legally set up the legal structure of the business in a manner that allows you and your entire family to participate in some of the benefits. In Chapter 15, we discussed some of the many tax benefits that result from having a small business, so feel free to refer back to that chapter for a very quick refresher course.

Business Strategy No. 1: Create Lifetime Income

The primary reason for building your own business is to create income for yourself. If you don't think you can do that, then don't go into business. The key, as we tell our children, is to *find something you like to do, and then figure out how to make money at it.* This isn't always easy to do. But if you can find a business that fits your mission, then it is more likely to be successful and profitable.

Another important aspect of building a business is to understand the difference between *building a business* and *creating a job for yourself.* A business is something that works for you. A job is a place where you work for a check. Big difference!

Business is like riding a bicycle—either you keep moving or you fall down.
—Anonymous

In his best-selling classic *The E Myth*, Michael Gerber talks about the frustration that many entrepreneurs face once they start to operate the business they've founded.

Many find themselves so involved in the day-to-day grind that they forget why they went into business in the first place. The freedom that they sought through having their own business is lost, and they are no better off than if they had a regular job working for someone else. Sadly, in some cases, they become *worse* off because of the added strain and responsibility they've taken on. Don't let this be you.

Business Strategy No. 2: Hire Family Members to Shift Income

Like all businesses, your small business will require many simple but often tedious tasks that have to be performed to keep it functioning properly. These tasks include cleaning your office (even a home office) and your office equipment, stuffing envelopes, running errands, performing basic data entry on the company's computer, and many other such tasks.

Hire your kids or grandkids to do the work, and pay them their allowance in exchange for the work they do. This way, the money you pay them becomes salary and, therefore, a tax deduction for your business. Obviously, the age of the child will determine what level of job you feel comfortable giving him or her, but even a young child can perform tasks like sweeping, vacuuming, and emptying trash.

Let's get an idea of just what sort of savings you can realize by having your child work in your business. Say you have a home-based business, with a room in your house dedicated to serving as a home office. You could pay your child $15 a week to clean and maintain

The youth of a nation are the trustees of posterity.

—Benjamin Disraeli

your office (you'd be getting off cheap), and nothing to perform the other tasks she or he may already do in the other parts of the house.

By dividing up the work explicitly as paid-for work done specifically on behalf of your business and work done as incidental household chores, you have now created a legitimate way by which you can deduct the cost of your child's allowance.

So, what does this deduction mean to you in savings? Take a look at an example, using our $15-a-week figure. At that rate, you will pay your child $780 in one year. If you are in the 27 percent tax bracket, then the amount of your deduction is determined by multiplying $780 by 27 percent (780 × 0.27), which comes to $210.60. So, by having your child work in your small business, you can deduct more than $200 of the $780 in allowance that you were probably paying your child anyway.

The most important thing to remember is that your children (or any other family members you hire) must perform the work for which they are paid. In addition, you cannot *overpay* for the work done. That isn't going to be a tough constraint, however, because you probably will not pay your kids more than the equivalent of minimum wage in the form of allowance.

If you were hiring someone other than a family member, you would have to pay *at least* that, so you're going to be fine. When you hire your children, you don't have to withhold federal taxes from their pay, or pay payroll taxes or Social Security until they turn 18.

What's more, you don't have to pay federal unemployment taxes on them unless they are 21. As far as the child's tax obligation on earnings, neither the child nor you owes anything on the money paid in wages, up to the amount of the standard deduction for single filers—which in mid-2005 is $4,750.

While you are gaining benefit from employing your children, they can also profit. Remember, the money you are paying them is now considered earned income. This means that your children, no matter their age, can start funding an IRA with this money. By starting an IRA years earlier than most, they gain more years of tax-free compounding (in a Roth IRA), which will accelerate the building of their retirement nest egg.

Even though there are exemptions, noted earlier, that make this a worthwhile strategy for both you and your child, you are *not* exempt from issuing your child an IRS Form 1099 that declares the wages paid. This is important, because without this official indication of what you paid, you will not be able to claim the associated deduction. Also, it is important to note, you do *not* lose the standard dependency exemption that you receive for having kids when you hire them for your business.

Although we have focused on the tax deductibility benefit of hiring your children to work in your business, there are other payoffs as well. If you aspire to one day have your small business serve as something more substantial to you and your family, then who better to hire (as soon as it is realistically possible) than the children who will probably take it over one day?

We've all heard the horror stories of family employees gone wrong, but the truth is that the majority of us trust few people more than we trust members of our own families. As previously mentioned, we ourselves have at least five members

> *Youth today must be strong, unafraid, and a better taxpayer than its father.*
>
> —H. V. Wade

of the family working together on various projects in our own business.

Additionally, hiring your children to work in your business can't help but foster in them a greater appreciation for the ideals of hard work, entrepreneurship, and money management. We have always found that those who began working at a young age demonstrate a greater level of maturity and business acumen than those who did not.

The simple reason for this is that the path we all take to a lifetime of employment and career management begins much earlier for these folks, and that this head start can make a big difference in the long run, in terms of both attitude and success.

Business Strategy No. 3: Use Your Business to Fund Your Retirement

For owners of a small, home-based business that runs profitably, one of the "nice problems" you face is what to do with your income. You certainly could go out and spend the money, and you *should* spend some of it in order to enjoy the benefits of all the work you're doing. You could also pour it right back into growing your business, and that's a good idea too, but if your operation is indeed small and home-based, it isn't likely that you'll be spending much on a regular basis.

One suggestion of what to do with the income is to use it as the source of funding for your retirement plan. The rules with respect to the various forms of retirement plans are such that those who are self-employed, even part-time, can put a lot more money into a retirement plan than regular employees can. This is the smartest use of income derived from a small business operated part-time.

Although there are a variety of retirement plans available to small businesses, the SEP (Simplified Employee Pension) IRA offers great benefits. The advantage of the SEP IRA for the owner of a small business, particularly one who has only himself or himself and just a few employees, is that it is an IRA with greatly expanded contribution limits.

While other retirement plans, like the defined-contribution and defined-benefit plans, have other benefits, it is likely that the SEP is going to fit your small business like a glove. The great thing about the SEP is that even though the cost and burden of plan administration is really no different from that of a regular (or Roth) IRA, you can contribute as much as 15 percent of your income, up to a maximum of $25,500 annually. This "skunks" the regular and Roth IRA annual contribution limit of (currently) $4,000 annually. And because they are small and easy to maintain, SEP IRAs can, like regular IRAs, be opened just about anywhere, giving you terrific flexibility in your investment choices.

Your strategy, then, is to use the income from your small business to greatly "power up" your retirement by setting up a SEP-IRA and contributing far more to it than you can to a regular IRA. If you really want to

Victory in the next war will depend on EXECUTION not PLANS.
—George S. Patton

maximize your retirement outlook, then continue contributing to your regular or Roth IRA or company-sponsored retirement plan *and* set up your SEP-IRA on behalf of your part-time, self-employed income.

The IRS permits you to maintain both plans simultaneously, and that reinforced assault on the future cost of retirement will ensure that you live comfortably for the rest of your days.

As your company grows and begins to make more money, you may want to consider adopting a defined-benefit retirement plan, which would allow you, and your employees, to decide how much money you would like to receive at retirement, and then fund that much money up to certain limitations. Depending on your age, there are also certain catch-up provisions that allow you to set aside large amounts of money because you got a late start in the retirement benefit area. This is a complex topic, but if your company is making a lot of money, then you can't afford not to look at these benefits and get them properly set up.

Business Strategy No. 4: Get Tax-Free Insurance Benefits

By forming a corporation for your business, you can also qualify for insurance savings. A corporation can deduct premiums for insurance payments, and since you are an employee, you can do this for yourself, as well.

Without the corporation, you and any other employees you have (including family members) would have to purchase insurance with after-tax dollars. This can amount to quite a benefit, depending upon your tax bracket. The insurance benefits you can receive apply to both health insurance and life insurance limited to one-year renewable term policies up to $50,000 per person.

Disability insurance is also deductible by the corporation. However, in this case, you may decide to pay for the insurance yourself. If you pay for it, then any insurance payments you get in the event of a disability are not income. But if the corporation pays for them, then the payments would be treated as income and be subject to income tax. Don't try to make a lot of sense out of the rule; it is just one of those things it won't pay to argue about.

If your corporation is a C corporation, then you, as an employee, can have a medical reimbursement plan. Most people do not get to deduct medical expenses because to be deductible, these expenses must be a high percentage of your adjusted gross income. Using the corporation and your small business, all of your expenses can be deducted.

Business Strategy No. 5: Conduct Business in Vacation Spots

We wrote earlier that business should be fun. And we are not the only ones who share that view. Jack Welch, the legendary former CEO of GE, said many times throughout his career that business should be fun, exciting, and exhilarating.

One of the best ways to have fun is to schedule your next big business meeting in a place you like to go. We have had board meetings in Hawaii and have enjoyed several cruises in which business seminars were held. Yes, there are guidelines you have to follow to make certain trips eligible, but that is OK.

You just have to take the time to structure these trips properly and make sure that you are acting within the tax code at all times. The key is to have a business purpose, and really conduct your board meeting or other business where you are. If you also have family members on your business board, they will be able to go as well.

> *He that can take rest is greater than he that can take cities.*
>
> —Benjamin Franklin

Business Strategy No. 6: Create Your Exit Plan

Another major benefit of building a business is that you are creating an asset that some day you can sell or leave to your heirs. If you sell the business, then the sale qualifies for lower capital gains treatment if you have held it for more than a year. There are a lot of people interested in buying successful businesses of all sizes, so this is not a pie-in-the-sky scenario.

If your business is a small business, you can sell it locally through a business broker. If it grows into a large and thriving business, there are bigger opportunities, such as a public offering or an outright sale to another company in the same line of business. Investment bankers handle these transactions, and their interest is determined by the amount of money your business makes and can continue to produce.

In either event, by venturing into the world of business, you open up new options for yourself that you would not otherwise have, and you can control your own destiny. Isn't that what financial freedom is all about?

YOUR MISSION TO WEALTH TO-DO LIST

1. CONSIDER SETTING UP A SMALL BUSINESS. All you need is an idea, a little seed capital, and determination.

2. CONSIDER TURNING THAT BUSINESS INTO A FAMILY BUSINESS. People hear horror stories about being in business with family members. We do it all the time. It's not horrible; it's great—if you take the time to structure it right.

3. LOOK FOR WAYS THAT THE BUSINESS CAN DO MORE THAN GENERATE A SALARY. Look for the tax breaks and other advantages that are associated with doing business within the family. Fund your retirement, pay insurance premiums, or take a cruise, all on the business—as long as you play by the IRS's rules, of course.

4. PLAN AHEAD FOR THE HARVEST. Too many entrepreneurs act as if (a) they're going to live forever and (b) they're going to take it with them. Neither is true. Start thinking early on about how you're going to get *out* of this business and take some of the value that you've created with you.

Index

★ ★ ★

About the Authors

★ ★ ★

JAMES DICKS, president and CEO of PremiereTrade™ LLC, a financial services company that specializes in brokerage services and financial services software, is an internationally renowned trainer and motivator. He has appeared on nationally syndicated radio shows and before international audiences, lecturing on personal finance, real estate investing, and the Foreign Exchange (FOREX) market. The bestselling author of *FOREX Made Easy: Six Ways to Trade the Dollar*, James served in the United States Marine Corps and is an active member of the Marine Corps League.

JW DICKS brings more than 35 years of professional experience in the financial industry to his readers and clients worldwide. JW is a securities attorney, registered investment advisor, licensed securities principal, licensed real estate broker, and chairman and chief corporate counsel of PremiereTrade™ LLC. He also operates a venture capital firm which has raised millions of dollars in start-up money for a number of financial, high-tech, and development companies.